EX·LIBRIS

Rev. George N. Vida

THE ESSENCE
OF ORTHODOX ICONOGRAPHY

CONSTANTINE D. KALOKYRIS

Professor of Christian and Byzantine Archaeology
University of Thessalonike

Translated by

PETER A. CHAMBERAS

Rev. George N. Vida

«Οὕτω καὶ σκεῦος ἕκαστον λέγομεν καλόν, καὶ ζῷον
καὶ φυτόν, οὐκ ἀπὸ τῆς διαπλάσεως οὐδ' ἀπὸ τοῦ
χρώματος, ἀλλ' ἀπὸ τῆς διακονίας».
(Χρυσόστομος)

"Thus, we say that each vessel, animal, and plant
is good, not from its formation nor from its color,
but from the service it renders."
(St. John Chrysostom)

BROOKLINE, MASS.

1971

CONTENTS

CHAPTER FOUR

MAIN DIRECTIONS AND PRESUPPOSITIONS FOR A RENAISSANCE OF ORTHODOX ICONOGRAPHY

PREFACE TO THE ENGLISH EDITION

The first edition of the present book was written in Greek five years ago in Athens, and within a very short period of time was sold out. The Greek public and several publishers have since requested its reprint, but I have delayed this because it is my wish to complete and to make my book more comprehensive by dealing with added aspects of Orthodox Iconography. Unfortunately, the multitude of engagements and the publication of my other books have not yet permitted me to do this.

While teaching Christian Archaeology this year, however, as a visiting professor in the United States at Holy Cross Greek Orthodox Theological School in Brookline, Massachusetts, I accepted the request of the student body and the faculty that a translation be made of my book in English, even under its present form. Thus, the present English edition makes its appearance and only in a few points differs from the first Greek edition. These points are mainly additions of more examples of icons in which the differences between Orthodox and non-Orthodox Iconography can be seen. Also, I have added more citations from the Fathers of the Church.

This desire of the faculty and student body of Holy Cross Greek Orthodox Theological School for the present translation was accompanied also by the profound conviction that, in an era of wide discussions regarding possible "dialogue," especially with the Roman Catholic Church, the Orthodox must in every respect make known to the brothers of all other churches in the West the content of our Orthodox Faith. It is certain that Roman Catholics and Protestants are in many ways still ignorant of us; they do not know well who we are and what we believe. Since for us Orthodox the Christian monuments usually project great religious truths and the art of the Church expresses always the Orthodox spirit, we regard it necessary that they understand the nature of Orthodox art and how we interpret it. The interpretation which we give to it is not subjective, that is, not in accordance with our personal tastes and desires or our idiosyncrasies and cultural background in general, but in accordance with the great sources of Orthodoxy, namely, the New Testament and the Fathers of the Church. Furthermore, those of us who know the Christian monuments, not

5

only from our study of books but also from personal excavations and restorations of them, can comprehend more precisely how much the Orthodox Christian art agrees with the Fathers of the Church. It is inconceivable for us to have art critics and historians of the West speak pretentiously concerning Orthodox art from a purely aesthetic point of view. Certainly, any good doctor can speak about surgery without being a surgeon. A surgeon, however, is one who opens human bodies, examines anatomically the organisms, and restores the function of ailing organs. Parallel, therefore, to the theory there must also be the practice. And thus, the Orthodox byzantinologists (unlike those philologists who merely repeat whatever they have learned from the non-Orthodox in the West) present the art of Orthodoxy as it is manifested in the Fathers and in the monuments which agree with them. Anyone, of course, may accept or may reject the authority of the Fathers. But when one desires to interpret seriously Orthodox art and especially the iconography of the Orthodox churches, it is not possible to overlook the Greek Fathers of the Church, for it was precisely their opinions and decisions (as individuals or as councils) which influenced fundamentally the formation of Orthodox iconography.

The present book, however, was not written for the heterodox only, but rather it is primarily directed to the Orthodox. Its main purpose is to direct the contemporary Orthodox away from certain heterodox influences in their present religious art and to convey to them the essence of Orthodox iconography. Of course, the writer is motivated by the realities of contemporary Greece. But these realities may have greater importance for Orthodoxy in general, granted that Greece possesses among her Byzantine monuments an iconography of unique significance.

For this reason, the author will regard this edition as successful if, on the one hand, it becomes a source of motivation for the unbiased heterodox to think seriously about Orthodox iconography, and if the Orthodox, on the other hand, come to understand it more fully and to work for the creation of other similar studies.

CONSTANTINE KALOKYRIS
University of Thessalonike

Brookline, Massachusetts
May, 1965

PROLEGOMENA

CONTEMPORARY GREEK ORTHODOX ICONOGRAPHY

Those of us who are occupied with Christian archaeology and art observe with much sorrow the misunderstanding which exists, not only among the Western ecclesiastical and theological circles but even among our own, in regard to the fundamental significance of the iconography of our Orthodox Catholic Church. In the West, of course, favorable voices on the part of byzantinologists have been heard and these have lately increased in number, just as it has happened on the part of the same circles in Greece. But the failure to understand the significance of our Orthodox iconography is a disturbing force among the more competent, who see in this iconography not merely an external or helpful element, but precisely an essential element of the worship in spirit of the Orthodox Church.

One cause of such a condition is the lack of appropriate research into the essence of Orthodox iconography and, consequently, of a relative bibliography on the part of Roman Catholic and Protestant Theology. After the Schism (1054) and mainly from the 13th century onwards, those who cultivated in the West a different type of iconography neglected in their theological studies the painting of the Eastern Church, which was little by little certainly connected with the depreciation of and the general antipathy toward Orthodoxy which followed the Schism. With the Renaissance, the prominence of Aristotle, and the humanist studies in the West, an anthropocentric art form developed and its ideal was imposed upon the Roman Church (and consequently upon the Protestant). This "new" art which the Roman Church adopted was one expression of her independence from the "one Church" from which she was separated. In the West, moreover, Byzantine painting has been studied only as part of the History of Art, or the History of Christian Art, or Christian Archaeology, or even the Philosophy of Art — sciences which examine their subject according to their presuppositions. As a result, the historians of art primarily and the aesthetes of the West speak about Byzantine art, while the strictly papal-ecclesiastical environment regards this art as strange to its "new tradition," which, naturally, it bequeathed to the Reformation. Thus, from an historical and artistic — in the usual sense — point of view, the usually generalized or even the rarely specialized bibliography does not concern us here, except indirectly. This significant bibliography, especially the more recent one, has contributed to the reappraisal of certain generalized false conceptions about Byzantine art and to the exaltation of its artistic worth in itself. It is disadvantaged, however, in that it examines rather the "form" (εἶδος), that is, the style of this art, while the "matter" (ὕλη), that is, the content or subject matter, is not examined fully, precisely because these scholars, worthy in other respects, are found outside Orthodoxy and do not know the essence of Orthodox iconography.

Another reason, related to the one above, for the lack of understanding Orthodox iconography, is the fact that certain literary and artistic circles, shaped within the European environment, have set up, according to an unjustified anachronism and a one-sided view of the variety of artistic forms, the classical ideal and the ideal of the Renaissance as the only criterion for the evaluation and devaluation of all art. Thus, through the tradition created by their authority, these circles have influenced the general conceptions regarding art and particularly iconography.

A third cause of the condition described above is the lack, on our part, of a specialized, living, and intense cultivation of the understanding in the nature, the character, and the particularity of Orthodox Byzantine iconography. We do not mean here, of course, certain praiseworthy movements for the publication of isolated studies or albums of especially colored Byzantine icons and paintings. This omission we localize in our Orthodox Church, in whose bosom there has not been developed the appropriate movement for the study and understanding of — as we shall see — the *liturgical, dogmatical, high spiritual,* and, generally speaking, *theological* significance of her art. For these distinctive characteristics, Byzantine Art remains an element of outstanding significance for Orthodoxy's tradition, which justly projects this and other constitutive elements in the contemporary Ecumenical Movement. The heterodox being far from our liturgical and other traditions, are ignorant or rather indifferent to the significance of Byzantine iconography. But the sad thing is that some of our own people, especially among the responsible leaders of the Church, have not fully familiarized themselves with its spirit. To this, at least, one is led by the existence still in Orthodox churches of icons which are anything else but of the Byzantine tradition, iconographies of a worldly artistic manner — demonstrating the non-existence of a higher artistic spirit. These works follow Western models or usually constitute such falsified copies, which are not only from the beginning unrelated to the sublime spirit of Orthodoxy, but also dogmatically suspicious, as we shall see. We attribute this fact certainly not to the intentions — anything but this—but to the false ideas about art, according to which an icon or a wall-painting of any merit is only one which depicts the persons naturally beautiful, one which renders their physical conditions naturalistically, one which records, according to the laws of perspective, the relation of the depicted persons to themselves, to the space, and in one word, one which shows the sacred scene according to any colored photograph.

Certainly not a little of the responsibility for these false ideas belongs to those later painters, who, either influenced or completely captured by the attraction of Western iconographies, transported them — there being no opposition — through their copies into our churches. Being unable to distinguish between the iconography of the West which adopted the methods of worldly art and the essentially ecclesiastical-theological art of Orthodoxy, which is represented by the Byzantine tradition, these men contributed much — especially from the time of the Independence of the Greek State — in causing the iconography of the Church to appear quite different from its traditional form. Of course, the intrusion of Western art into our iconography is much older. The borrowed elements were originally limited to the externals and not to the essence of the iconography, being assimilated under the strong personality of an iconographer — as seen in their works which manifest a unity of form. The borrowed elements begin to become evident, however, after the Fall of Constantinople (1453), and especially from the 17th century on. Our sacred painting, technically, stylistically, and iconographically was hitherto — more or less according to areas — influenced by the West. A serious reason for this influence was the enslavement of the Greek Nation by the Turks. This created a great drawback to the general education, and thus, on the one hand, the appropriate evaluation of the heterodox art, the enlightenment, and the necessary opposition of our Church was not possible, while, on the other hand, the related manifold Western propaganda was favored. This propaganda through art, which by no means was insignificant since it concerned *the character of Orthodoxy's Tradition,* was not perceived, it seems, or at least was not seriously opposed by the Orthodox Church. The copper engravings of Western artisans which circulated widely during the entire Turkish domination (especially in the Venetian held Ionian Islands and in such islands as Crete and Cyprus), the icons of a clearly Western character, and the lithographies especially from Italy which unfortunately flooded the country after the independence of Greece — with which the pupils of our Catechetical schools were only until recently supplied, or are supplied even today — constitute, we think, an undoubted proof of this unfortunate condition. We observe also this paradox: while during the entire period of slavery we had western influences in our iconography, there existed, nevertheless, iconographers who observed the tradition either strictly or inoculated in it (with discretion) borrowed elements, such as did not change its whole atmosphere. (Be it noted especially that in Crete, despite the Venetian rule, the complete lack of bishops and well educated priests, and despite the strong propaganda of Roman Catholicism, especially after the Council of Florence, the wall-paintings of hundreds of churches remained strictly faithful to the Byzantine tradition.)[1] On the contrary, after the Independence of the State, when the foreign pressure disappeared and the Church was reorganized, not even a word was spoken about Byzantine iconography in Greece.[2] The first painters after the Independence and those who followed them, being trained in the West or by others who were trained there and undergoing also the "imposition" of the foreigners in Greece (Thirsch, Seitz), followed the current of the foreign iconography, which was to "correct" (!) the Byzantine models on the basis of the European art.[3] Even on that most sacred palladium of Byzantine art, that is, the Holy Mountain Athos, instead of reviving the old art of Panselenos (14th century, Protaton) and of Theophanes (16th century, Lauvra), who created incomparable compositions from a qualitative viewpoint, the so-called "painting of the Iosaphaioi" appeared over seventy years

---

[1] See C. Kalokyris, Αἱ Βυζαντιναὶ Τοιχογραφίαι τῆς Κρήτης [The Byzantine Wall-paintings of Crete] (Athens, 1947), p. 177.

[2] The Italianization of the iconography of the Ionian Islands preceded, but finally this iconography which is strange to the Greek Orthodox sentiment declined.

[3] To "correct," that is, to distort, because this is precisely what actually happened.

ago. This new style constituted not only a decline artistically,[4] but also a sign not at all pleasing to the Church because of the unprotested diversion of the tradition in this center of Byzantine civilization, which is most significant for our Orthodox Church.[5]

Fortunately, this whole grievous situation has been opposed during the last decades in Greece by certain iconographers (not merely painters) who, having understood the value of Orthodox iconography, have turned toward it wholeheartedly. And it is extremely satisfying to see their studios increase day by day. Thus, Byzantine and post-Byzantine sacred art is beginning to be revived and promoted, even if its promotion is done without an indicative system and a particular method, or even if it meets with some opposition. But the recent wall-paintings done in certain cathedrals and other centrally located churches in Greece, as well as the placing in many other churches of certain portable icons of an Orthodox style, undoubtedly constitute the good beginning, honoring our Church, toward the reunification of tradition and τὸ ἀρχαῖον κάλλος ἀναμορφώσασθαι (the reformation of the ancient beauty) of this art. Because this art, for which this movement is struggling, demands spiritual cultivation to be understood, there still exists the misunderstanding which sees it in the same way as the secular painting and evaluates it according to its own criterion. For this reason — especially since this concerns a fundamental element of Orthodox Tradition — it is necessary to do everything possible in contributing to the removal of this misunderstanding which still exists among many out of ignorance. It is, therefore, necessary to inform ourselves as well as the non-Orthodox. This is the purpose which this study sincerely intends to serve by undertaking, along the more principal lines, the analysis of the essence of Orthodox iconography. At the same time, this study expresses a joy, for contemporary Orthodoxy is again following this sacred art's revered tradition.

---

[4] This was a type of iconography which on Mt. Athos was developed by the Monk Ioasaph from Asia Minor and his pupils, and which was influenced by the lithographic Russian icons and the whole climate of the 19th century regarding the "correction" of Byzantine painting according to the aesthetic notions of European art.

[5] Today (1965) we rejoice in making known that the present Iosaphaioi have also turned to the Byzantine tradition. See C. Kalokyris, Ἄθως, Θέματα Ἀρχαιολογίας καὶ Τέχνης [Athos. Themes of Archaeology and Art] (Athens, 1963).

CHAPTER ONE

THE CONTENT OF ORTHODOX ICONOGRAPHY

«Οὕτω καὶ σκεῦος ἕκαστον λέγομεν καλόν, καὶ ζῷον καὶ φυτόν, οὐκ ἀπὸ τῆς διαπλάσεως οὐδ' ἀπὸ τοῦ χρώματος, ἀλλ' ἀπὸ τῆς διακονίας».

(Χρυσόστομος)

"Thus, we say that each vessel, animal, and plant is good, not from its formation or from its color, but from the service it renders."

(St. John Chrysostom)

The knowledge of the content of Orthodox iconography is indispensable. This knowledge is necessary not only for the evaluation of the subject matter itself, but also for the understanding of the form, that is, the external characteristics which express that which we call the style of iconography. The knowledge of the content of iconography is the knowledge of the purpose for which this art has been consecrated. Without this purpose in mind, it becomes impossible to evaluate the character and the fundamental significance of this sacred art.

1. *Art of Spiritual Service.*

The purpose of iconography in the churches was, from the beginning, one: service to the Church. Iconography appeared as art not for its own sake, but for the Church. Thus, its content was determined directly by the needs and the profounder purposes of the Church. These purposes, of course, were not material but spiritual, purposes which the Church had to proclaim by every possible means. The foundation of faith in the spiritual reality, in the immortality of the soul and in the blessedness that is in God was primary. The pursuit of blessedness in the present temporal and in the future eternal life was to be achieved by participation in the Mysteries and by the life the faithful would go through in observing all that Holy Scripture and its official interpreter, the Church, commanded. The believer had to be taught in every way possible that, in his journey toward perfection in Christ, he would have to struggle against the powers of darkness, against manifold evil, and even to reach martyrdom, as did the Saviour, the Apostles, and the Martyrs of the Faith. It was necessary for the Church to present these personages as examples to inspire, to guide, and to encourage the faithful. In the life of the Church there were also misinterpretations of the

13

orthodox teaching that she followed, that is, heresies emerged. For this reason, the Church established her Creed, her dogmas. For these and about these, the Church developed the higher Theology. From the pulpit this Theology was exposited and interpreted. But besides these dogmas, there was need — especially for the simpler folk — of other more empirical commentaries. Later on, to that very house where the faithful assembled, to the church building, the Church added the meaning of the «ἐπιγείου οὐρανοῦ ἐν ᾧ ὁ ἐπουράνιος Θεὸς ἐνοικεῖ καὶ ἐμπεριπατεῖ» (earthly heaven wherein the heavenly God dwells and walks about).[1] This must be apprehended in a more perceivable manner by the multitudes who enter the church.

For all these purposes, i.e., her needs and her aspirations, the Church sought the assistance of painting. And in all those purposes, only Orthodox iconography of all periods responded completely. Thus, the content of the iconography was interwoven with *the life, the evolution,* and *the whole tradition* of the Church, so much so that a knowledge of this tradition will certainly be incomplete without a knowledge and understanding of iconography. During the early centuries, when the persecutions required that the Church be careful in the expansion of her ideas, painting served perfectly this purpose through her *symbols.*

Under the simple symbols of the fish, the lamb, the shepherd, the heart, the peacock, the vineyard, the anchor, etc., the pure hearts of the believers of the early era understood the ideas of greatest significance of the new Faith, such as hope, salvation in Christ, resurrection, and immortality. Later, after the triumph of Christianity, when the Church wished to express her formation in history and the redemptive work of Grace continuing in her, the iconography from symbolical became historical, that is, it interpreted the historical content of the triumphant Faith. The Saviour and the events of His life, the Theotokos, the Saints and the Martyrs constituted the great epic of the «ἱστοριῶν» ("histories") of the Christian churches. Later on again, after the iconoclastic controversy and the victory of Orthodox belief regarding the icons and the official bond of Orthodoxy with iconography (the victory of the icons was regarded for this reason as a victory of Orthodoxy and it is as such that the Sunday of Orthodoxy has

---

[1] Patriarch Germanos, Migne, P.G. 98, 384.

14

been named in commemoration), the painting was characterized as dogmatic, since its content dealt with the doctrinal truths. The Pantocrator in the dome depicts at once the Father and the Son — the expression of the dogma concerning consubstantiality. The dogma of the Virgin as «ὄντως Θεοτόκου» (truly Mother of God), formulated by the Council in Ephesus (431), was expressed characteristically, after the iconoclastic controversy, by consistently portraying the Mother of God and the Child Jesus on her knees in the quarter-sphere of the niche canopy, in the Sanctuary. The dogma of the first and second Coming of the Lord was expressed by the presentation of the «'Ετοιμασία» (preparation of the Throne) with the empty Throne of Judgment and the instruments of the Passion of the Saviour in the vault before the apse of the Sanctuary. Finally, from the Macedonian and Comnenian period (10th-12th century), the development of the monastic spirit, the cultivation in it of the ecclesiastical literature, and the study of the apocryphal writings, gave the content to the contemporary iconography, which, especially during the period of the Palaeologoi (13th-15th century), became a *narrative* art. The iconographic compositions, from this period on, became richer and contained many persons; psalms and hymns (such as the Akathistos Hymn) as well as many scenes from the Apocrypha, were depicted in the churches.

But let us see these things more specifically. As we said, the faith of the Church in the reality beyond this world, that is, in the truth of the spiritual world, defined from the beginning the essential character of the content of her iconography. She is primarily interested in the beauty of this spiritual world and, with the means which she possesses, the Church seeks to be the interpreter of that world. But because this spiritual world is not visible but is expressed, the particular painting of the church does not present her themes, but simply expresses them. Her transcendental content is not the physically beautiful or the naturally good; and for this reason does not seek to project natural good and beauty (τὸ κατὰ φύσιν καλόν). Those, therefore, who see and judge Byzantine iconography with the conceptions of classical antiquity regarding the beautiful, will only confuse things. The purpose and the ideal of ancient Greek art was the projection in the presentation of the natural good and the beautiful by nature in that well known undivided unity of καλὸς κἀγαθός (beauty and virtue). On the contrary, the purpose and the ideal of Byzantine iconography is the expression of the category of holiness, which, of course, is not made sensate by the physically beautiful, that is, is not by necessity united to this. In antiquity the ideal was shown by the formation of things according to the laws of the naturally good. For this reason, Plato in his *Politeia* taught the artists: «τὸ ἄσχημον μήτε ἐν εἰκόσι ζῴων μήτε ἐν οἰκοδομήμασι μήτε ἐν ἄλλῳ μηδενὶ δημιουργημένῳ ἐμποιεῖν . . . ἀλλ᾽ ἐκείνους ζητητέον τοὺς δημιουργοὺς τοὺς εὐφυῶς δυναμένους ἰχνεύειν τὴν τοῦ καλοῦ τε καὶ εὐσχήμονος φύσιν». (The ugly should not be depicted in the images of living things nor in structures or any other created things . . . but those creators (artists) must be sought who are intelligently capable of tracing the things which are by nature beautiful and graceful.)[2] On the contrary, in the Christian Orthodox art the beautiful is not determined from the natural formation of the objects, but from its *sublime content,* that is, from its power of serving the ideals of the Faith. This is characteristically confessed by St. John Chrysostom: «Οὕτω καὶ σκεῦος ἕκαστον λέγομεν καλὸν καὶ ζῷον καὶ φυτὸν οὐκ ἀπὸ τῆς διαπλάσεως, οὐδ᾽ ἀπὸ τοῦ χρώματος, ἀλλ᾽ ἀπὸ τῆς διακονίας». (Thus, we say that each vessel, animal, and plant is good, *not from its formation or from its color,* but from *the service it renders.*)[3] Thus, the sublime purpose, the content of a superior spiritual quality concerns the Church, which regards as good any work whose formation, color, and form in general can express this content. And, in this connotation, the works of Byzantine iconography have undoubtedly been proven as good. This art did not copy nature nor seek the form or the color as an end, but, taking such technical and artistic elements as were necessary for the believers to become familiar with its spirit, succeeded, through an exceptional abstraction, in rendering the more sublime meanings of Orthodoxy.

2. *Liturgical Art.*

We have already noted the significance given by the Church to her Mysteries and their relation to the salvation of man. The position of the Mystery of Holy Eucharist in the Church is also known from the beginning as it constituted the center and the essence of the Liturgy, which is but a representation of the Mystery of the Divine Economy. The fundamental significance of the

---

[2] *Pol.* 401 B. f.
[3] Migne, P.G. 11, 253. Homily 4 on I Timothy.

Holy Eucharist is not only unequivocally stated by the Fathers, but also manifested by Christian art in its most ancient monuments. The assembly of the believers in the church takes place primarily for the experience of the represented work of salvation in Christ and for the participation at the Τράπεζαν Κυρίου (Lord's Table), to which the prayers, the hymns, and the sermon are directed. The liturgical act of the priest is a repetition of the one done in Heaven by Christ, the Great High-Priest.

Iconography was placed from the beginning at the disposition of this highest purpose of the Church. It became a *liturgical* art. It sought to contribute with its own means to the believers' understanding of the great mystery of Holy Eucharist and of the whole liturgical drama. At first in the Catacombs the «'Ιχθύς» (fish) was presented, which, together with its other significance, was the symbol of the Holy Eucharist, since him «ἐδράξατο Παρθένος ἁγνὴ καὶ τοῦτον ἐπέδωκε φίλοις ἐσθίειν διὰ παντός» (a pure Virgin grasped and him did give to friends *to eat* forever), according to the famous inscription of *Avercius of Hieropolis* (2nd century).[4] In the Catacombs of Alexandria the same mystery was marked by the representation of the multiplication of the bread and the fish.[5] The Lamb again, a favored subject of Christian art, was «τὸ ἐσφαγμένον» (the slaughtered) lamb of Revelation,[6] «τὸ αἴρον τὴν ἁμαρτίαν τοῦ κόσμου» (bearing the sins of the world) through its sacrifice.[7] Early in the Catacombs and later in the churches[8] the representation of the three young men in the fiery-furnace, of Daniel in the lion's den, and especially of the sacrifice of Abraham were considered as symbols of the eucharistic sacrifice and were represented in the Sanctuary, which, as it is known, is related to the heavenly Altar. Later, especially from the era of the Macedonian and Comnenian emperors, the representation of the «Θεία Λειτουργία» (Divine Liturgy) was consecrated for the niche in the Sanctuary depicting the Great High-Priest, Christ, below a ciborium (permanent canopy over the Holy

---

[4] Dölger, ΙΧΘΥΣ, vol. 2 (1922), pp. 252 f.

[5] Millet, in Michel's *Histoire de l'art* (1905), p. 192.

[6] Revelation 5:5.

[7] John 1:29.

[8] As in the Catacomb of St. Callistus in Rome, etc. or in the Church of St. Vitalius in Ravenna.

Table) — rarely only once, but more commonly twice[9] transmitting on one side His Body and on the other side His Blood to the Apostles who in order or, as later, in groups approach with awe. But later still the Divine Liturgy was represented in this space in its other ideal performance in Heaven, that is, the Sacred Gifts are carried in litany by the angels wearing the vestments of deacons and are presented to the Great High-Priest, the Lord, as we have it in that excellent wall-painting in the Perivleptos church of Mystra (14th century). Below the Divine Liturgy are depicted the «σεβίζοντες» (venerating) great Hierarchs (especially from the Palaeologian period) with their liturgical scrolls (they are the editors of the Divine Liturgy). These personages are inseparably related with the depicted mystery, a fact which was made more emphatic from the 12th century onwards by the presentation of the sacrificed Lamb upon the Paten, which later became the Μελισμός, that is, the painting of the Lord as a child in this vessel (divided into pieces) and alluding to the sacrifice of the Lamb performed by the Priest on the Holy Table.

The liturgical themes mentioned above: the Communion of the Apostles, the Liturgy of the Angels, the «θυόμενος» (the self-sacrificing one) and the co-celebrant Hierarchs before Him, as well as the older ones, such as the sacrifice of Abraham, etc., determine especially the so-called *liturgical* iconographic cycle which, with the two other cycles (that is, the dogmatic and the cycle of Feast days) dominate in the Orthodox churches from the Byzantine period. Thus, the *liturgical* content is one of the principal characteristics of the essence of Orthodox iconography.

When the Church calls us who «τὰ χερουβὶμ μυστικῶς εἰκονί- ζοντας» (represent mystically the cherubim) to «πᾶσαν τὴν βιω- τικὴν ἀποθώμεθα μέριμναν» (abandon every worldly concern) in order to receive the King of all who is invisibly escorted by angelic orders, Orthodox iconography comes to help more empirically in making this invitation as well as the whole purpose of the cherubic hymn more conscious. The ideal figures of the angels represented in the Byzantine churches, who approach with awe as they bear the Gifts to the Great Hierarch Lord, and the Apostles, depicted in utter contrition and compunction, who come

---

[9] Once, as in St. Sophia of Ochrid (11th cent.); twice, as in St. Sophia of Kiev (11th cent.), etc.

to receive communion from His immaculate hands, make perceptible the content of the hymn in truly the best manner and impose with their whole spiritual atmosphere its understanding. No art ever succeeded in expressing what was expressed by the Orthodox art in Mystra. Here, in the famous wall-painting of the Perívleptos Church,[10] the fleshless figures of the angels (plate 35) in a magnificent rhythmic procession, bearing with fear and trembling the Sacred Gifts, and covering their views before the highest Sacrifice, offer to the spectator, through the achieved dematerialization, the impression of a vision from the other world and make incomparably perceptible the content of the liturgical hymn: «Σιγησάτω πᾶσα σὰρξ βροτεία καὶ στήτω μετὰ φόβου καὶ τρόμου καὶ μηδὲν γήϊνον ἐν ἑαυτῇ λογιζέσθω . . .» (every human keep silence and stand with fear and trembling and think not of any earthly thing concerning thyself). Truly, the technique and the style of inspired Orthodox iconographer — as we shall see more specifically in the following chapter — with the whole formation of the persons with a few lights upon the chestnut-colored first color and with the ethereal movements of the bodies, succeeded in commenting excellently upon the magnificant hymn and in exalting the believers to its liturgical height. Even if one is not familiar with such things, he needs but to compare these angels of Mystra (14th century) — to limit ourselves only to these — with other angels of the then contemporary painters in the West, such as, for example, those of Simond Martini (beginning of 14th century), Lippo Memmi, A. Orcagna, and even those of Cimabue and Giotto (end of 13th century) in order to understand what is expressed by such figures of Byzantine art. These latter artists copied handsome and naturally beautiful models of young men and, from the point of view of their art, may be worthy works as faithfully rendering or beautifying the models according to nature, but nothing more. On the contrary, the former artists, avoiding the models of natural beauty, created works of a marvelous spiritual quality, figures that are truly celestial, intensely expressive of the profound liturgical life which filled their whole being.

From what was presented above, we think, the significance of

---

[10] See Millet, *Monuments byzantins de Mistra* (Paris, 1910), illustration 113.

Orthodox iconography has become apparent as a liturgical art, aiming to make understandable and conscious to the faithful the sublime content of the Divine Liturgy and especially of the profounder liturgical act of the Holy Eucharist.

3. Art of High Theology.

Orthodox Byzantine iconography is not simply a religious art, as in the West, but also *theological*. Its themes are not simply related to religious history, but are organized according to the high Theology of the Orthodox Church. In the West there is no such order, but everything is mixed together; religious canvasses of famous painters of the Renaissance, often unrelated with each other, decorate the churches. Usually the Roman Catholic churches are decorated with the pictures of the Passion of Christ, which are related to the known "stations" of the Roman Church (le chemin de croix). Thus, the whole church is filled with the Passion, one-sidedly and exclusively emphasized, while in the doors of the churches, the Church receives her faithful with the fearful scene of the Second Coming.[11] On the contrary, the Orthodox Byzantine churches are filled with the twelve scenes of the great feasts from the whole life of Christ, the known «Δωδεκάορτον» (Twelve Great Feasts).[12] Thus, not only the Passion is emphasized, but the all embracing life of the Lord, including the main events in His life from His Birth until His Ascension. In other words, the high theology of Divine Economy is represented, which, certainly, is not only the Passion.

The Twelve Great Feasts represented in the vaults of Byzantine churches, fill the architecturally formed cross of the vaults and display to the faithful in its entirety the earthly life of the Saviour. Whatever is taught by the Divine Liturgy, by the hymns of the Church and the words from the pulpit, is ex-

---

[11] See e.g. the related relief representations of the great, especially Gothic, cathedrals of France, such as those of St. Stephen in Meaux, of the Virgin Mary in Amiens, of St. Peter in Angouleme, of St. Lazarus in Autun, of the Virgin (north gate) of Reims, of the Virgin of Strasburg, and others. Cf. D. Rops-Yvan Christ, *Cathédrales de France* (Paris, 1952), pp. 13, 16, 24, 41, 45, 48.

[12] Regarding its formation in the 11th century see offhand G. Millet, "L'art byzantin," in Michel's *Histoire de l'art* (Paris, 1906), p. 196 (Daphni). Cf. also Millet, *Le monastère de Daphni* (Paris, 1899).

cellently commented upon by the silence of iconography. For this reason St. Gregory of Nyssa said most characteristically: Ζωγρα-φία σιωπῶσα ἐν τοίχῳ λαλεῖ πλείονα καὶ ὠφελιμώτερα, (While silent on the wall, painting speaks many and more useful things). The cross of the vaults especially, which covers the church and which depicts within its four sections the whole life of the Saviour, offers the impression to the faithful standing below that they are dominated by that sacred symbol *par excellence,* that they are under the protection of the Κυριακοῦ σημείου (the Lord's Sign),[13] which contains and expresses all Christian teaching.[14] At the entrance of the church, at the βασίλειον πύλην (Royal Gate) the faithful are received by Jesus, τὴν θύραν (the door),[15] that is, by the Lord as Teacher,[16] being represented above the entrance looking forward, blessing and bearing the Gospel on which is inscribed ἐγὼ εἰμὶ ἡ θύρα (I am the door), or ἐγὼ εἰμὶ τὸ φῶς τοῦ κόσμου (I am the light of the world),[17] or ἐγὼ εἰμὶ ἡ ὁδὸς καὶ ἡ ἀλήθεια καὶ ἡ ζωὴ (I am the way and the truth and the life),[18] as we have, for example, in the mosaic (9th century) of St. Sophia in Constantinople[19] and in the mosaic of Hosios Loukas (11th century) near Levadeia, Greece. Later on, in the dome which rises at the center of the church and at the point where the vaults cross, the triumphant figure of the Pantocrator, the Lord ἐξομολό-γησιν καὶ μεγαλοπρέπειαν ἐνδεδυμένος (clothed in praise and magnificence), dominates over the entire area and is illumined by the abundant radiant light which enters from the windows in the drum of the dome. As the Pantocrator is projected from the depths of the dome, the center of the cross formed by the vaults appears to be hollowed and extended by Him to the infinite, as if to denote that this central point of the Cross is the triumph of the Resurrection, that its essence and depth is the Victor over death, the Infinite Lord, who dwells in Heaven καὶ τὰ ἐπὶ γῆς

---

[13] According to Clement of Alexandria, *Stromates,* 11, in Migne, P.G. 8.
[14] Ὁ λόγος τοῦ Σταυροῦ (the word of the Cross), according to St. Paul, I Cor. 1:18.
[15] John 10:9, Ἐγὼ εἰμὶ ἡ θύρα· δι' ἐμοῦ ἐάν τις εἰσέλθη σωθήσεται (I am the door; if any man enters through me, he shall be saved).
[16] Matthew 23:8.
[17] John 12:34, 46.
[18] John 4:6.
[19] Grabar (Skira), *La Peinture Byzantine* (Géneve, 1953), p. 97.

ἐφορῶν (and supervises the things of earth), the immortal King of all to whom πᾶν γόνυ κάμψῃ οὐρανίων καὶ ἐπιγείων καὶ καταχθονίων (every knee shall bend in heaven and on earth and below the earth).[20] Actually the dome became for the Byzantines the symbol of Heaven, while the Pantocrator, as already noted, was more specifically ὁ Πατὴρ ἅμα καὶ ὁ Υἱὸς (The Father and the Son together), the expression of the doctrine of their consubstantiality. More generally speaking, we must see three other attributes which the Byzantine Pantocrator expresses. He is *the Creator, the Saviour*, and *the Judge*.[21] This triple theological significance is successfully conceived and excellently rendered by Orthodox iconography. Thus, the Byzantine Pantocrator possesses the royal magnificence of the Creator, the expression of the active goodness of the Saviour, and the austerity of the impartial Judge.[22] Even here the art, serving the ideals of the Church, created a work of great power which expresses a whole Theology (Creation, Salvation, Judgment). And it is as expressions of this theological thought that the Pantocrators of Orthodoxy should be regarded (see e.g. the Pantocrator of Daphni, or of the Ὄμορφη Ἐκκλησιὰ (Beautiful Church) in Patesia, Athens); their value should certainly not be measured by the naturalistic notions regarding the art of the West. It becomes clear then that only iconographers who understand Byzantine art, both technically and stylistically and who have strong Orthodox convictions, are able even today to create similar works.

In the quarter-sphere of the niche in the Sanctuary of Orthodox churches, the Theotokos is usually depicted holding the Child Jesus and escorted by two archangels. This quarter-sphere, with the rest of the niche, is the architectural section which unites

---

[20] Philippians 2:10.

[21] Related to these three attributes of the Pantocrator are the various epigrams of which one may be inscribed around Him. The epigram ἴδετε, ἴδετε ὅτι ἐγώ εἰμι . . . (See, see that I am . . .) refers to the Creator; ἐπίβλεψον ἐξ οὐρανοῦ (Look down from heaven . . .) refers to the Saviour, while the ἰδοὺ Θεός τε καὶ κριτὴς πάντων πέλω (Behold the God and judge of all comes . . .) refers to the Judge.

[22] It is the expression of the *good-will* (because of which God ἐξ οὐκ ὄντων εἰς τὸ εἶναι παρήγαγε τὰ σύμπαντα (from non-being brought all things into being), of the *highest love* (because of which God was incarnate and saved man), and of the *divine justice* (for whose restitution He will return in glory).

the roof of the church with the floor; the upper (dome), symbolizing the heavens where the Pantocrator is represented, is united with the lower, that is, the earth, the floor of the church, where the faithful are standing. Here, therefore, the Theotokos stands between heaven and earth, as ἡ μεσιτεύσασα τὴν σωτηρίαν τοῦ γένους ἡμῶν (the intercessor for the salvation of our race), as ἡ κλῖμαξ ἡ ἐπουράνιος δι' ἧς κατέβη ὁ Θεὸς (the heavenly ladder by which God descended), as ἡ τὰ ἄνω τοῖς κάτω συνάψασα (the one who united the upper with the lower) by means of the Divine Child in her arms.

The representation of the Lord as Teacher at the entrance of the church, the Pantocrator in the dome, and the Theotokos in the niche of the Sanctuary determine the so-called *dogmatic cycle* of iconography in the Orthodox Church. The high Theology which this cycle, together with the other two, expresses will be sought for in vain outside the Orthodox Church.

In the churches of the West, the foggy and melancholy atmosphere is in agreement with the whole iconography there.[23] On the other hand, in the Orthodox churches the abundant light, which enters from the many windows in the walls and in the dome, περιαστράπτει τὴν ἐκκλησίαν (makes the church glitter), and one can say that it becomes the symbol also of the Orthodox iconographic perceptions. The light, the symbol of life, of joy, and of the Resurrection,[24] praised by our Church as an expression of her διαρκὲς Πάσχα (perpetual Easter), her continuous joy of the Resurrection,[25] which is emphasized and praised by Orthodoxy each Sunday in her early morning Gospel reading, in the Praises, in the Glory hymns and in the whole Liturgy, certainly outlines also the resurrectional character of the iconography. The

---

[23] Because of their architectural design with the multitude of arches, iconography was not favored especially in the Gothic churhces, resulting in stained glass windows.

[24] Cf. δεῦτε λάβετε φῶς ἐκ τοῦ ἀνεσπέρου φωτός (Come receive ye light from the never-setting Light . . .).

[25] The Gospel reading also for Easter emphasizes that Christ ἦν τὸ φῶς τὸ ἀληθινόν, ὃ φωτίζει πάντα ἄνθρωπον ἐρχόμενον εἰς τὸν κόσμον (was the true light which lighteth every man who cometh into the world), John 1:9. Cf. also the known hymn ἡ 'Ανάστασίς σου Χριστὲ Σωτὴρ ἅπασαν ἐφώτισε τὴν οἰκουμένην . . . (Thy Resurrection Christ Saviour gave light to the whole world). Regarding the joy of the Resurrection, Christ said that οὐδεὶς αἴρει ἀφ' ὑμῶν (no one shall take away from you), John 16:22.

icon of the Resurrection of the Saviour, with the magnificent scene of the descent into Hades (in which He is represented in the midst of luminous glory) (plate 14), His appearance to the two Maries (in the midst of a bright springtime landscape), the scene of the women before the tomb and the angel dressed in white and totally enveloped in light (ἦν δὲ ἡ ἰδέα αὐτοῦ ὡς ἀστραπή . . . and his countenance was like lightning),[26] and, finally, the scene with Peter and John at the tomb, certify by their variety this characteristic of Orthodox iconography. But in this respect, it may also be said of these icons that they are a commentary upon the rich resurrectional hymnography of the Church, expressing her profounder theology in relation to the great and invincible event of the Christian Faith.

Related to the high Theology of the Church is also the whole content of Orthodox iconography. This content concerns the καινὸν οὐρανὸν καὶ καινὴν γῆν (the new heaven and the new earth) of Christ's redemptive work, the man and the world of regeneration. It is not concerned with the "old," "the natural," the transient. That is to say, Orthodox iconography represents the world regenerated by divine Grace, the world where the unsetting light of God dominates. The citizens of such a world are the saints and the martyrs; and the success of Orthodox art lies precisely in the fact that it has succeeded in making manifest this world of Grace; but, of course, only as far as the available means make it possible. To this purpose it resorted to accommodating presentations, as we shall see. Orthodox art is not concerned with natural human form except "as an expression of a thought and of a faith" (Lemerle). This line is followed by the Orthodox iconographer, who thus does not work like the secular painter. Iconography is not personal, that is, it does not express the personal understanding of the artist; rather it seeks to express in art the significance of the events of divine Revelation. Besides, personal opinion in art does not usually coincide with the total or overall conscience of the Church; whereas Orthodox painting has an *ecumenical* character and seeks to express the creed of the μιᾶς, ἁγίας, καθολικῆς καὶ ἀποστολικῆς ἐκκλησίας (one holy, catholic and apostolic Church), which is its only authority. When we speak about the "personality" or the "personal style" of the Byzantine

---

[26] Matthew 28:3.

iconographer, we do not do so in the usual manner, that is, with reference to the personal, original interpretation of the form of an iconographic theme. In speaking about the "personality" and "personal style" of the Orthodox artist, we mean his power to express through his artistic tools, more profoundly and more clearly than his other colleagues, the spiritual ideals of the Faith.

We have said that Orthodox iconography exalts the world of Grace and the divine reality beyond this present world. Persons participating in the world of Grace within the Communion of Saints are represented in one manner; persons participating in Grace but living still in this world are represented in another manner; while those who are deprived of the spirit and Grace are also depicted in another manner. To the first, the artist gives infinite spirituality, reduces the mass and the weight, that is, the elements which remind one of the material. Behold, for example, the holy martyrs and the holy women in the mosaics of the middle aisle of the new church of St. Apollinarius in Ravenna (6th century). In the green fields of Paradise the martyrs and the holy women, dressed in white and gold garments respectively, and being liberated from weight, with their gaze fixed on infinity and wholly divinized, approach in orderly procession to deposit the crowns of their martyrdom which they bear in their hands, the men before Christ and the women before the Theotokos.[27] In contrast, the mosaics depicting Justinian and Theodora with their retinues in the church of St. Vitalius within the same city, denote in the tense characteristics and the formation of the faces that they still live in this world.[28] Likewise in St. Sophia of Constantinople, the mosaic in the balcony depicting the Theotokos between John II Comnenos and his wife Irene (12th century), shows the Mother of God with the Child Jesus in ideal form, while the persons of the living imperial couple are shown with their actual and natural characteristics.[29] Also in the Aphentiko

---

[27] Grabar, *La peinture Byzantine,* pp. 54, 55.

[28] *Ibid.,* pp. 62, 63.

[29] Grabar, *La peinture Byzantine,* pp. 96, 97. And in the monastery church of Milecheva in Serbia (about 1235), for example, the angels are depicted in a different manner from the King of the Serbians Vladislav, who, as a living person, is shown with all the characteristics of his individuality. See Oto Bihalji-Merin, *Fresques et Icones* (München, 1958), illustrations 31, 32.

(Odeyitria) church of Mystra, the martyrs represented in a choir are works of a high supra-personal expression, while, by contrast, Theodore II Palaeologus constitutes a true portrait painting.[30] The same can be said regarding the outstanding forms in the Monastery of Chora (Kahrie Djami) of Constantinople in relation to the face of the great prime-minister (logothetes) Theodore Metochites. Suffice it to mention only these few examples.

The exact opposite is true of the religious — but not theological — art of the West. Criminals and saints, sinful women and the immaculate Theotokos, mortal men and the immortal Lord, are represented in the same manner by the same naturalistic art. In the wall-painting, for example, of the Second Coming in the chapel Strozzi of Santa Maria Novella in Florence, which is the work of A. Orcagna (1350), the condemned are in no way differentiated from the elect, not even the Judge Christ and the Virgin from the people below. The characteristics of natural men are common to all.[31] Even in the canvas of Raphael (1560), representing the Transfiguration and the incident of the Gadarene daemoniac, which hangs in the Art Gallery of the Vatican[32] (a copy of which is suspended upon a column in the church of St. Peter in Rome), there is no difference whatsoever depicted, as regards the naturalistic execution of faces and clothing, between the Jewish crowds on the one hand and Moses, Elijah, the Apostles and even the Lord on the other. The same is true with the Second Coming in the Cappella Sistina of the Vatican, a work of Michelangelo, where the interlocking robust figures of the righteous and the condemned, together with the technical and stylistic uniformity of the whole composition, give the impression of a struggle of Giants, related, one could say, to the statuary compositions decorating the metopes of eaves of an ancient Greek temple . . .[33] Only with great difficulty could one see a real difference in form between Christ and the Jew pointing at Him in Derick Baegert's "Christ before Pilate" in Nuremburg.[34] The whole atmosphere of the canvas is purely human. In the West

---

[30] Millet, *Monuments byzantins de Mistra* (Paris, 1910).

[31] See at random J. *Fattorusso, Florence* (Florence, 1952), p. 75.

[32] J. Mesnil-Braun, *Raphaël* (Paris), illustration 60.

[33] G. Poggi (Astra-Arengarium), *Michelangelo* (Firenze, 1951), illustrations 53, 54, 55, 56.

[34] H. Lützeler, *Icons of the Saviour* (Freiburg, 1944), Illustration 12.

only Theotokopoulos (El Greco), because of his origin and roots in the Byzantine tradition, which undoubtedly is potentially hidden in his work, shows through his best canvases the differences between the spiritual and the material world, as we see, for example, in the "Dream of Philip II," "Martyrdom of St. Maurice," "Burial of Count Orgath," and others. This is true especially in the "Crucifixion" at the Louvre (1584-1586), in which the two brothers Covarrubias[35] stand worshipping at the feet of the Crucified Christ. Here Christ in his whole image, the successful lighting, and the nobility of his face, is intensely contrasted from the brothers below, who constitute two naturalistic and actual portraits. Nevertheless, despite such exceptions, Western iconography as a whole, laboring under the anthropocentric outlook of the Renaissance, did not succeed, even with its abundant means of expression, in achieving the difference between the two worlds, as Orthodox iconography truly succeeded in expressing with its simplicity.

4. Orthodox Iconography as an Art of Depth.

Totally characteristic of the content of Orthodox iconography is its depth. It is evident that a spiritual, a liturgical, and a theological art, as we have seen, should have sought to express depth and profundity in the representation of its themes. It is for this reason precisely that it neither impresses, nor does it capture those who habitually limit themselves to the surface of things. Those who, willingly or unwillingly, still regard this art with the impressionistic presuppositions of the 19th century, are making a serious mistake in choosing their critical method.

It is not possible for one with the presuppositions of an extrinsic impressionistic art to examine and to judge an iconography, which by its very nature is expressionistic. This is the reason why this art began to be understood among the limited circles of Europe when Expressionistic Art succeeded Impressionistic Art.[36] People began to realize that the essence of art is not lim-

---

[35] See at random G. Rouchès, *Greco* (Paris, 1950), illustration 21. Also C. Kalokyris, Θεοτοκόπουλος ὁ Γκρέκο [Theotokopoulos, El Greco] (Athens, 1965).

[36] Mauchair, *L'impressionisme, son histoire, son ésthétique, ses maîtres* (Paris, 1903), pp. 16 f. Cf. also R. Hamann, *Der Impressionismus in Leben und Kunst*, 1907.

ited to the brilliant colors and the impressions which the eye receives, but in addition to these, is more so the ἐσωτερικὴ ἐντελέχεια (inner perfection), the artistic "expression" of a profounder life-experience which possesses the soul of the true and genuine artist. Thus, for example, the Germans realized little by little the significance of the expressionism of their medieval art, which had been set aside by the art of the Renaissance. Also the Orientalists understood the expressive value of the closed forms of Egyptian art. The historians of primitive and ancient cultures also understood the importance of such art as Minoan expressionism. A good examlpe of this is the large eye of the so-called «Παρισινῆς» (Parisienne).[37] Thus, finally, the artistic circles began to understand Byzantine art with its intense features (e.g. the large eyes, the large noses, such as those of the Theotokos), the bright contours, the frontal postures of the saints, etc., which express its depth, that is, the content of Christian dogma and spirituality. The large eyes and the other characteristics animated, beyond measure, interpret the entire intensive psychical life of the represented persons. The frontal attitude of the saints again denotes the direct communion between these sacred personages and the faithful.

Being, therefore, an expressionistic art of profound significance, Orthodox iconography is not directed only to the sentiments, but also, and primarily, to the spirit. It does not seek to make a momentary and passing impression, but to create a permanent and continuous influence upon the soul by means of the understanding and practice of its content by the faithful. Indeed one Western icon of the Lord, for example, the so-called "Blond Nazarene" (sic), with hair parted in the middle of the head and falling to the shoulders in uniform waves, with blue eyes, with the musing or melancholy countenance of 18th century romanticism, and the whole naturalistic rendering of the figure, is directed perhaps, through the passion for beauty, to the emotion of certain people. But the flabbiness, the languor and lack of any

---

[37] See N. Platon, *Führer durch das Archaelogische Museum von Heraklion* (Herakleion, 1958), illustration XII. For the above presuppositions of a turn to Byzantine expressionism see my article Νεώτεραι Πρόοδοι τῆς Χριστιανικῆς καὶ Βυζαντινῆς Ἀρχαιολογίας ["New Advances in Christian and Byzantine Archaeology"], reprinted from Θεολογία, vol. 31, A (Athens, 1960).

expressive power of such pictures does not move those who seek spiritual satisfaction, that is, those who seek under the expressive figures the shattering and profound idea of the icon, just as happens with the Byzantine icons of Christ in which the exuberance of the characteristics (such as the large eyes and the searching spirit) and the whole vigorous expression render, in the best possible manner, the majestic and exalted spiritual nobility of the Lord's face.[38]

What we are saying becomes clearer when we examine the Crucifixion icons of Western art in contrast to similar icons of Byzantine iconography. The Western art presents here a tragic drama of a man undergoing the ultimate agony of suffering. It is primarily directed to the emotions and seeks to move one by exalting human pain. And so Western artists compete to see whose work will be more dramatic. They depict, therefore, the opened mouth of the Crucified-One in its final death spasm. They encircle the head with an excessively large crown whose sharp thorns pierce low on the forehead. They drip clots of blood on the half-opened but effaced eyes. With the picture of the horror of a human corpse (cadaver) they seek the creation of "sympathy" (Einfühlung) — in the artistic sense — in the spectator. Some examples of this, among many others, are the "Crucifixion" of Granach (1472-1553) in the Gallery (Haus der Kunst) of Munich;[39] the "Crucifixion" of Fernandez (1566-1636) in the Museum of Valladolid;[40] the "Crucifixion of Goya (1746-1828) in Madrid (Prado);[41] and especially the "Crucifixion" of Grünewald (died 1530) in the church of Isenheim,[42] where the tragedy of the suffering Christ is climaxed by the moribund spasm displayed by the projecting teeth from the opened mouth and the

---

[38] Such Byzantine icons of Christ can be seen in A. Xyngopoulos, Κατάλογος τῶν Εἰκόνων τοῦ Μουσείου Μπενάκη [Catalogue of Icons in the Benaki Museum] (Athens, 1936), illustrations 14 no. 17, 15 no. 19, 33 no. 44; and in G. Sotiriou, Ὁδηγὸς τοῦ Βυζαντινοῦ Μουσείου [Guide to the Byzantine Museum] (Athens, 1956), illustrations XVI, XVII, XX. and p. 23.

[39] See H. Lützeler, op. cit., illustration 15.

[40] H. Lutzeler, op. cit., illustration 23.

[41] Ibid., illustration 14.

[42] This crucifixion comes from one of the two polyptichs in the altar of the church of Isenheim. See also H. Möhle, Das Antlitz Jesu Christi im Wandel der Zeit, pp. 19-21.

foaming tongue.[43] These scenes are, after all, in agreement with the hymnody of the West and especially of the Protestant Churches. Thus, the above unsurpassed realistic cruelty of Grünewald's Crucifixion recalls immediately to mind verses from the choral hymn of Bach's "Passion of Matthew":

> O Haupt voll Blut und Wunden,
> voll Schmerz und voller Hohn!
> O Haupt, zu Spott gebunden
> mit einer Dornenkron! . . .[44]

Furthermore, Crucifixions of the type of Grünewald in Isenheim (now the Museum of Kolmar) as well as in the Gallery of Art in Washington (the so-called little Crucifixion) indicate the complete διαφθοράν (decomposition), the dissolution, distortion, and putrefaction of the body due to death. One who examines the above Crucifixions of this painter will verify that the body of Christ has the green color of decay!

By contrast to the above Crucifixions of Western art, in the Orthodox Eastern art, the iconographers were not concerned only for the emotion but for the whole being of the believers. Thus, they created icons of the Crucifixion in which, in the face of the Lord, royal majesty (the majesty of controlled passion), calmness and serenity dominate and express, instead of the pain of martyrdom, the sublime theological significance of the completed Sacrifice upon the Cross, which is condensed in Christ's word τετέλεσται . . . (it is finished, that is, His work is completed). Thus, while the Western painter, directing his work to the emotions, presented a human drama, the Orthodox iconographer, directing his work primarily to the spirit, expressed τὴν ἐν σταυρῷ θείαν κένωσιν (the divine *kenosis* or emptying on the Cross) of the God-Man. Moreover, the Orthodox painter, believing with the Fathers and the hymn-writers of the Church that the flesh of the Lord did not suffer any decay whatsoever (ἡ γὰρ σάρξ σου διαφθορὰν οὐκ οἶδε δέσποτα "for thy flesh Lord knew no decay"),

---

[43] "Die weissen Lippen sind im Todesschrei erstarrt und lassen Zähne und Zunge sichtbar werden . . ." It is confessed that the suffering man is presented: "Es bleibt alles im Raum des Menschlichen; die Knechtsgestalt höchst schimpfieret, ohne Heiligenschein . . ." *Ibid.*, p. 20.

[44] "Matthäus-Passions," Textbuch, Breitkopf and Hartel (Wiesbaden), p. 13.

represented the body of the Saviour without any change on account of death. The body of the Lord διὰ τὸν ἐνοικήσαντα Λόγον ἄφθαρτον διέμεινε (remained incorruptible because of the indwelling Logos), according to St. Athanasius the Great.[45] For this reason there are neither spasms of the mouth here nor effaced eyes; the color of the body is not made greenish-yellow, nor distorted. The calm incline of the head and the closed eyes are sufficient in great art.[46] Only an art deprived of content and expressive power resorts to external and secondary elements in order to impress and to impose itself through them. An art, however, which has the power to express profundity avoids such superficial elements (even if often these have an historical character). This is done in order to avoid any change in its essence through them. Moreover, ὁ Ἐσταυρωμένος ἅπαντα ἀταράχως ἔπραττε (the Crucified-One did all things imperturbably), according to St. John Chrysostom.[47] Outstanding works of such expression are, among many others, the Crucifixion of Daphni (11th century),[48] of Hosios Loukas near Levadeia (11th century),[49] of the reliquary of Cardinal Bessarion (15th century) found in the Accademia of Venice,[50] of the Monastery of Lavra on Mount Athos — a work of Theophanes of Crete (1535),[51] of the Museum of Zakynthos — a work of Michael Damascenos (end of 16th century), and the Crucifixion of the Byzantine Museum in Athens.[52]

---

[45] Migne, P.G. 25, 112.

[46] In Orthodox art, the body of the Lord is bent, and even more so during the Palaeologian period, in order to show that the body is dead and is bent by its weight.

[47] Migne, P.G. 59, 461.

[48] Millet, Le Monastère de Daphni (Paris, 1899), illustration XVI.

[49] E. Diez-O. Demus, Byzantine Mosaics in Greece: Hosios Lucas and Daphni (Cambridge, Mass., 1931), illustrations 99 f.

[50] Millet, Recherches sur l'Iconographie de l'Évangile (Paris, 1916), illustration 478. Cf. Lazaref, History of Byzantine Painting [Russian] (Moscow, 1948), vol. II, illustration 350.

[51] Millet, Monuments de l'Athos, I, Les Peintures (Paris, 1927), illustration 129, 2.

[52] G. Sotiriou, op. cit., p. 30 and illustration XXIIIa. Cf. also from the same Museum the Crucifixion no. 169 of the 14th century, ibid., p. 17, illustr. XIX. Exceptional Crucifixions besides the known ones of Mount Athos (Millet, ibid., illustrations 12, 3; 69, 2; 83, 2; 129, 2, etc.) in wall-paintings of the 14th to the 16th centuries see C. Kalokyris, Αἱ Βυζαντιναὶ Τοιχογραφίαι τῆς Κρήτης [The Byzantine Wall-paintings of Crete] (Athens, 1957), illustrations XIV, XV, XVI, XVII.

In Orthodox art, not only the person of the Lord manifests in death a high nobility, but also His Mother and the disciple John, who are represented standing by the Cross in controlled grief. Moreover, according to George of Nicomedeia (9th century), the Theotokos τῷ πάθει κοσμίως καὶ οὐκ ἀγενῶς προσωμίλει (spoke at the Passion modestly and not ignobly).[53] But even later when the related scenes were enriched and the realistic theme[54] was introduced, wherewith the Theotokos was represented lamenting, pulling her hair, overcome with grief, and fainting by the Cross,[55] this had a purely narrative character, even though it was expressed by the contraction of her eye-brows, or by raising the hand to her head, or finally by the support of her body by the myrrh-bearers. And yet it does not come to any stylistic excesses which change the entire divine atmosphere of the icon. These scenes belong primarily to the realistic art during the period of the Palaeologoi. When regarded within the whole realm of the related icons, they do not bear the character of servile imitation of the natural reality. This means that they do not represent the facts according to the standards of the Renaissance, because the Orthodox painters succeeded in making their realism (a phenomenon proportionate to that in the sphere of ecclesiastical poetry and literature in general)[56] entirely refined and subservient to the more generally transcendental climate of their compositions, which dominated and placed its stamp in everything, as we shall see more specifically in the appropriate place.

Whatever is true regarding the difference between Western and Orthodox art in the presentations of the Crucifixion is also true in the representations of the Resurrection. In the Resurrection icon according to the impressive Latin type — created in the

---

[53] Migne, P.G. 100, 1485D. See in this connection the excellent Crucifixion of Daphni.

[54] About the realism in Orthodox art see in the following chapter.

[55] The reasons for this see in C. Kalokyris, *The Byzantine Wall-Paintings, op. cit.,* p. 72, note 1.

[56] In contrast, for example, to the Theotokos of George of Nicomedeia, who «θερμοτάτοις μὲν κατέλουε δάκρυσι», but «πραείᾳ φωνῇ καὶ συμπαθεστάτοις προσεφθέγγετο ῥήμασιν . . . [washed with warmest tears and with meek voice and with most sympathetic words did address the body of her dead Son] (Migne, P.G. 100, 1488), the Theotokos of Theophanes of Cerameus (Migne, P.G. 132, 597C) and of the hymn-writer of Great

11th century in the West[57] and made known through Giotto —
the Lord is represented holding a banner of victory as He is raised
in air as if by a vigorous jump from a sarcophagus tomb, whose
slate covering is raised by an angel, obviously to permit Him to
exit, while the guards are shown fallen upon the ground. Undoubtedly, this type seeks the lively impression of the spectator
by seeing the Saviour at the moment when He comes out
of the grave, while below the guards lie as if dead from
fear. But according to the Byzantine type, the Resurrection,
from the 9th century on,[58] is shown primarily by Christ's descent
into Hades. This iconographic type represents the Lord in Hades
surrounded by a radiant glory;[59] He is trampling upon the demolished gates of Hell and bears in His left hand the Cross of
the Resurrection, while with his right hand He raises from
a sarcophagus Adam (plate 7), who represents the human race.
Often, below the broken gates, one can see stretched out and
bound in chains the personification of Death as an old man,
whom the Saviour θανάτῳ πατήσας (defeated by death), while

Friday, standing by the Cross, ἀνέκραξε γοερῶς . . . ὀδυρομένη μητρῷα
σπλάγχνα . . . παρειὰς σὺν θριξὶ καταξαίνουσα . . . καὶ τὸ στῆθος τύπτουσα
(cried out mournfully . . . lamenting maternal bowels . . . wearing away
the cheeks together with the hair . . . and striking the breast), *Triodion*
(Venice edition, 1891), p. 395.

[57] H. Schrade, *Ikonographie der christlichen Kunst*, I, Die Auferste-
hung Christi (Berlin-Leipzig, 1932), pp. 43 f.

[58] Cf. C. Kalokyris, *The Byzantine Wall-Paintings*, p. 75, note 9. In
the formation of this type, besides the Palestinian tradition, there was a
contribution of the Ecclesiastical literature, such as Epiphanios of Cyrou
(see *Angerotos*, Migne P.G. 43, 77; *Against Heresies, ibid.*, 41, 276), the
Apocrypha (Tischendorf, *Gospel of Nicodemus*, pp. 328 f.), and the
hymnography (see *Triodeon* (Venice, 1897), pp. 413 f. Σήμερον ὁ ἅδης
στένων βοᾷ . . . ἐλθὼν γὰρ ἐπ᾽ ἐμὲ (ὁ Χριστὸς) τὸ κράτος μου ἔλυσε, πύλας
χαλκᾶς συνέτριψε . . . (Today, Hades bemoaning cries: for (Christ),
having come upon me, has abolished my power and demolished the brass
gates).

[59] According to the Apocrypha, *op. cit.*, p. 328, εἰσῆλθεν ὁ βασιλεὺς
τῆς δόξης . . . καὶ πάντα τὰ σκοτεινὰ τοῦ ἅδου ἐφωτίσθησαν (the King of
glory entered and all the dark things of Hades were illumined). Accord-
to the bishop of Caron, Theodore Aboukaras (8th century), the soul of
the Saviour γυμνὴ ταῖς ἐν σκότει ψυχαῖς ἐνδημήσασα, καὶ τὸ φῶς αὐταῖς τὸ
τῆς θεότητος ἀπαστράψασα . . . (visited in nakedness with the souls in
darkness and radiated the light of divinity to them), Migne, P.G. 97,
1496. Cf. also Nicephoros Kallistos, *ibid.*, 145, 724-5.

He Himself ἀνέστη (was resurrected).[60] Behind Adam are pictured Eve, Abel, the Forerunner, and others, while on the other side David, Solomon, and other kings and righteous men of the Old Testament are shown.[61]

In contrast to the Latin type, the Byzantine Resurrection clearly expresses a more profound spiritual content. It renders incomparably the profound significance of the victorious Hymn of Easter:

Χριστὸς ἀνέστη ἐκ νεκρῶν, θανάτῳ θάνατον πατήσας
καὶ τοῖς ἐν τοῖς μνήμασι ζωὴν χαρισάμενος,

(Christ was risen from the dead; He defeated death by death, and to those in the tombs He gifted life). This hymn declares that Christ, through His descent into Hades, defeated τὸν τὸ κράτος ἔχοντα τοῦ θανάτου, τοῦτ' ἔστιν τὸν διάβολον (him who has the power of death, that is, the devil),[62] and by His Resurrection He liberated and resurrected the dead of old and redeemed the entire human race — living in darkness and death — whose symbol is the forefather Adam.[63] The Orthodox type, therefore, expresses, like the Resurrection of Jesus Christ, a universal redemption,[64] that is, the work of salvation completed through the descent into Hades and the Resurrection following the victory over Hades. Thus, the Resurrection is not merely, as in the Latin type (exit from the grave), a visible declaration of that very instant in time only, when the event of rising from the grave took place.[65] As the Descent into Hades, the Byzantine

---

[60] On the descent of Christ into Hades, from a dogmatic viewpoint, see the truly "classical" study of Professor John Karmiris, Ἡ εἰς ᾍδου Κάθοδος τοῦ Χριστοῦ ἐξ ἐπόψεως Ὀρθοδόξου [Christ's Descent into Hades, from an Orthodox Point of View] (Athens, 1939).

[61] Cf. also G. Sotiriou in Ἀνάπλασις, 46 (1963), pp. 115-6.

[62] Hebrews 2:14

[63] Cf. the hymn for Vespers in mode Β΄ . . . τὸν Ἀδὰμ παγγενῆ ἀναστήσας ὡς φιλάνθρωπος (as lover-of-man thou raised Adam with the entire race).

[64] Cf. also from the hymnody τοὺς ἀπ' αἰῶνος δεσμίους ἠλευθέρωσας, ἀφθαρσίαν δωρούμενος τῶν ἀνθρώπων τῷ γένει . . . (you liberated those who were captives for ages and granted incorruptibility to the race of men . . .).

[65] For the manifestation of the event of the Resurrection in the visible world, that is, for its more empirical representation, the Orthodox iconography has the type of the Myrrh-bearers by the tomb, where the ἐξαστράπτων ἄγγελος (shining angel) sits, (ὁ λίθος).

type became very popular and was generally presented as the
'Ανάστασις (Resurrection) during the entire Byzantine period,
and even after the Fall of Constantinople (1453).

The Western type showing Christ jumping out of the grave
was imposed upon Orthodox iconography during the Turkish
domination (especially from the 17th century),[66] through the
influence of the West. It practically became the prevalent icon
of the Resurrection, when in essence it is a type not only untra-
ditional but unorthodox. It shows the Saviour rising from the
grave after the angel has moved the large rock for this purpose.
But the removal of the rock ἀπὸ τῆς θύρας τοῦ μνημείου (from the
entrance to the tomb), which is mentioned as a known fact by
all the Evangelists (Matt. 28:2; Mark 16:4; Luke 24:2; John 20:
2), was certainly not done so that the Almighty Lord could
emerge from the grave, but precisely so that the Myrrh-bearers
and the Apostles could see the empty tomb and verify the Resurrection. According to the Orthodox faith, the Lord was resurrected θεοπρεπεῖ δυνάμει καὶ ἐξουσίᾳ (by divine power and authority) while the tomb was still closed.[67] Moreover, οὐδὲ κεκλεισμέ-
νον ἦν τι τῷ ποιητῇ (there was not anything shut to the creator),[68]
as we are further reminded characteristically by the hymn-writers:

Κύριε, ὥσπερ ἐξῆλθες ἐσφραγισμένου τοῦ τάφου,
οὕτως εἰσῆλθες καὶ τῶν θυρῶν κεκλεισμένων πρὸς
τοὺς μαθητάς σου,

("Lord, as thou camest out from the sealed tomb, so also didst
thou enter while the doors were shut to thy disciples");[69]

Ἐσφραγισμένου τοῦ μνήματος ἡ ζωὴ ἐκ τάφου
ἀνέτηλας Χριστὲ ὁ Θεός . . .

("While the tomb was sealed thou didst rise from the grave
Christ the life, the God . . .")[70]

---

[66] The oldest example of such an icon of the Resurrection showing
Christ exiting the sarcophagus tomb we have in the Byzantine Museum
and is by E. Moskos, dated 1657. See G. Sotiriou, *Guide, op. cit.*, ed. B',
p. 88, no. 273. It is interesting to note that this artist only a few years
later (1670) returned to the Orthodox Tradition by painting the icon
of the Descent into Hades, now kept in the Benaki Museum. See Xyngopoulos, *Catalogue, op. cit.*, p. 37, illustration 23.

[67] Cyril of Alexandria, Migne, P.G. 76, 1165.

[68] Athanasius the Great, Migne, P.G. 25, 140.

[69] *Pentecostarion* (Venice edition), p. 130.

[70] *Ibid.*, p. 23.

And as John Damascene noted in the sixth ode of the Paschal Canon:

Φυλάξας τὰ σήμαντρα σῶα, Χριστέ, ἐξηγέρθης
τοῦ τάφου, ὁ τὰς κλεῖς τῆς παρθένου μὴ λυμηνάμενος
ἐν τῷ τόκῳ σου,

("Preserving sound the seals (of the tomb) oh Christ, thou didst rise from the grave, thou who didst not destroy the locks of the Virgin in thy Birth.")[71]

John Chrysostom also taught that μετὰ τὴν ἀνάστασιν ἦλθεν ὁ ἄγγελος . . . διὰ τὰς γυναῖκας. Ἵν᾿ οὖν πιστεύσωσι ὅτι ἠγέρθη, ὁρῶσι τὸν τάφον κενὸν τοῦ σώματος. Διὰ τοῦτο ἀνῆλε τὸν λίθον . . . ("After the resurrection the angel came . . . for the women. In order that they may believe that He arose, they see the tomb empty of the body. For this reason, did He remove the rock.")[72]

Gregory of Nazianzus, finally, also noted clearly:

ὃς (Χριστὸς) ἐξαναστὰς κειμένου λίθου τάφῳ,
καὶ τῶν σφραγίδων ἐμμενουσῶν εἰσέτι . . .
τὰ πάντα κατηύγασεν.

And added below:

Πῶς, πῶς, πάρεστι τῶν θυρῶν κεκλεισμένων;
τάχ᾿ ὡς ἀνέστη καὶ τάφου κεκλεισμένου, καὶ
πρὶν προῆλθεν ἐκ πυλῶν τῆς Παρθένου, ἄλυτα τηρῶν
κλεῖθρα μητρὸς παναγνου;

("While the rock lay upon the tomb and while the seals were still there, Christ arose and illumined all things." — "How, how is He present, the doors being shut? Just as He certainly arose while the tomb was sealed, and, before that, as He came forth from the gates of the Virgin, preserving unbroken the locks of the all-pure mother.")[73]

It would be a blessing, therefore, if this Western icon of the Resurrection, being actually unhistorical, simply impressionistic and essentially unorthodox, were to be abandoned, and the icon of the Descent into Hades were to be restored in our Church exclusively, according to her revered tradition. Compromises to the

---

71 *Pentecostarion*, p. 3.
72 Migne, P.G. 58, 783 (Homily in Matthew).
73 Migne, P.G. 38, 311 (The Suffering Christ).

detriment of Orthodox Tradition of worship and doctrine *are in no way whatsoever permissible.* And there may be perhaps some non-ecclesiastical and non-theological circles who are fond of the artistic syncretism of forms and themes and who consider this lawful and permissible in art. But the Church, which is not a museum or a picture gallery where heterogeneity and variety of forms is acceptable, must never and in no way accept anything that is essentially contrary to the strictly homogeneous and uniform tradition of her holy Orthodoxy. Famous representations of the Descent into Hades such as the one in Daphni, in Hosios Loukas, in the mosaics and wall-paintings of the Palaeologian period (e.g. of the Holy Apostles in Salonika, of the one recently discovered by the American Institute in the Monastery of Chora — Kahrie Djami, Constantinople) found in the monasteries, and in the many portable icons of these monasteries and of other collections — all these then can become models of inspiration for the Orthodox iconographers. Under the direction and care of the Orthodox Church these iconographers would work to re-introduce this type of icon, which constitutes one of the most fundamentally dogmatic art compositions through which Orthodox iconography is proved to be an art of depth (plate 7).

The same difference between Orthodox and Western art appears also in the presentations of the Birth of Christ, the Baptism, the Last Supper, etc. In the genuine Byzantine icons of the Birth, for example, the Theotokos only is pictured in the middle of the composition with the divine child in the manger; Joseph has no place here, but only afar off in a lower corner on the left or the right of the icon (plate 4). This is done to show that Joseph did not participate in the divine Incarnation of the Lord. The only persons who participated in the Incarnation were, according to Orthodox Theology, the Mother who offered the flesh (the body), and the Son who was incarnated in her by the Holy Spirit. In the icons of the West, however, Joseph is pictured in the cave and precisely together with the Theotokos, often kneeling just as the Virgin is opposite him.

In the Baptism of Byzantine painting moreover, Christ is pictured naked and within the water (plates 3, 9). A certain hymn of the Orthodox Church says: Γύμνωσιν αἰσχίστην περιστέλλων ᾿Αδὰμ τῷ προπάτορι, ἀπογυμνοῦσαι ἑκουσίως . . . ("In dressing the most disgraceful nakedness of Adam the forefather, thou didst strip thyself willingly"). By contrast, in Western art the Lord wears

37

a loin-cloth, because the painters did not understand the symbolism of nakedness. In Orthodox painting, Christ is immersed in the water of the Jordan River and is baptized by the Forerunner ἁπτόμενος τῆς κορυφῆς τοῦ Δεσπότου (by touching the head of the Lord), according to an appropriate hymn. Unlike this Byzantine Baptism, the Western icon depicts Christ so that he usually does not stand within the water but by some rocks, while the Forerunner pours upon His head water from a cup. We have here an expression of the baptism by sprinkling in the Roman Church (per imfusionem), while the Orthodox icons remind us of the baptism διὰ καταδύσεως (per immersionem), in agreement with the Catechesis of Cyril of Jerusalem.

Again, in the Orthodox icons of the Last Supper, a large fish is pictured in the plate before Christ and not a lamb. This is not so because at the Last Supper they did not eat lamb, but because the Orthodox icons are lifted beyond the historical event and become a symbol of the Holy Eucharist, calling us to ξενίας δεσποτικῆς καὶ ἀθανάτου τραπέζης ἀπολαύσωμεν (enjoy a royal hospitality and an immortal food). As it is known, the fish is the symbol of Christ, the θυόμενος (one being sacrificed) καὶ διδόμενος εἰς βρῶσιν πιστοῖς (and being offered as food for the faithful). Thus, the icon of the Last Supper uplifts the mind to the ψυχοτρόφον τράπεζαν (the soul-nourishing table) of Holy Eucharist, to Christ who is for us the καινὸν Πάσχα (new Pascha) (plates 1, 15).

5. Relationship to Ideal and Natural Models.

In the present general examination it is not without purpose to recall Pseudo-Dionysios the Areopagite (5th century), according to whom the Church should be regarded as a type and an image of the heavenly Church.[74] According to this understanding, all things in the Church allude to the heavenly world, and so it follows that even the painting must not represent forms of the daily life, but should express the spiritual and transcendental world. We have seen that this idea had already become, from the early centuries, a fundamental principle of Christian art. From this point of view, even Greek philosophy, especially the neo-Platonic, created a favorable climate for the further understanding of such a Christian ideal in art. Plotinus, for example, in

---

[74] Migne, P.G. 3, 369 f.

his "Enneads" had spoken about the vision of the world διὰ τῶν ἔσω ὀφθαλμῶν (through inner eyes), by which the profounder essence of things becomes understood, such as τῆς ἀρετῆς ἡ θεοειδὴς ἀγλαΐα (the deiform splendor of virtue),[75] a thing which does not occur in the mere external impressions achieved through the bodily eyes. According to Plotinus, knowledge should not be analytical and partial, but whole and direct, achieved through the vision of the true nucleus of things. But this nucleus, of course, which determines the entelechy forming the beings, is not related to the temporary and transient, or to the natural reality directly observable by the senses.[76]

In agreement with the above, therefore, Orthodox iconography avoided the representation of the sacred forms according to the natural reality and sought, through a truly marvelous abstraction upon these forms, to express *the spiritual reality* which constitutes its highest truth. For this reason, iconography did not use certain models of men, with which to represent its sacred personages by copying them systematically. We have already noted this above (no. 2, Liturgical art) in connection with the angels of the Divine Liturgy in the Perivleptos church of Mystra. But here we must see this more specifically in order to emphasize, even from this point of view, the qualitative difference between Orthodox and Western art. We shall insist on the two most important persons of iconography, that is, Christ and the Theotokos. Christ is hymned by the Orthodox as ὁ ὡραῖος κάλλει παρὰ πάντας βροτούς (the one of perfect mature beauty (spiritual) surpassing that of all mortals), as having τὸ θεῖον καὶ ἄρρητον κάλλος (the divine and ineffable beauty), etc.; the Theotokos is reverently said to be περιβεβλημένη θείαν χάριν, τοῖς ὄμμασιν ἁγιολαμπὴς καὶ ... ὅλη καλὴ (surrounded with divine grace, shining with holi-

---

[75] *Plotini Opera*, ed. A. Kirchhoc, vol. I-II, Lipsiae MDC CLVI, vol. I, p. 11, 9 (about the good).

[76] Ἡμεῖς δὲ τῶν ἔνδον οὐδὲν ὁρᾶν εἰθισμένοι οὐδ' εἰδότες τὸ ἔξω διώκομεν ἀγνοοῦντες ὅτι τὸ ἔνδον κινεῖ. (We, therefore, who are used to seeing nothing of the inner things, nor to know them, seek the externals, not realizing that it is the inner which moves.) *Ibid.*, vol II, ch. XXVIII, 25 (about poetic beauty). And below (34) he notes characteristically: ἀλλὰ πᾶσαν μορφὴν ἀφεὶς διώκῃς τὸ εἴσω κάλλος αὐτοῦ (but leaving every form seek ye its inner beauty).

ness and being all-beautiful to the eyes),[77] the ἁγία, ἁγίων μείζων (the greatest of all the saints) and ἡ μόνη ἄμωμος ἐν γυναιξὶ καὶ καλὴ (the only immaculate and beautiful among women), who amazed the archangel with τὴν ὡραιότητα τῆς παρθενίας καὶ τὸ ὑπέρλαμπρον τῆς ἁγνείας (the beauty of virginity and the brilliance of purity). Now, it would be outright impious to represent Christ and the Theotokos according to the natural beauty of some ordinary persons. For this reason, Orthodox art created for both of these persons those *idealized* types, in which the emphasis and elevation of the characteristics remove one from the physiognomies of everyday life and impose the idea of the transcendental reality to which they belong (plates 17, 18, 19). Thus, no model, no type of man exists to inspire in the Orthodox artist the sacred forms of the Saviour and of His Mother. Certainly those who are far from the spirit of this ideology of Orthodoxy find it difficult to understand why these persons are represented with supranatural characteristics and specifically large eyes, nose and hands. But those who understand more deeply the Orthodox artistic ideal, become capable of appreciating the effort of the Orthodox iconographer, who attempts to express the ὑπὲρ φύσιν, ὑπὲρ λόγον, καὶ ὑπὲρ ἔννοιαν (supra-natural, supra-rational, and supra-conceptual) elements of these divine persons through the ὑπερβολὴ (hyperbole, exaggeration), ὑπέρβασιν (excess), and even the παραμόρφωσιν (deformation) of the natural reality.

In contrast to this line of Orthodoxy, the Ecclesiastical art of the West, not aiming at the depth but at the surface of things, formulated types for the most sacred personages based on certain actual models. Thus, "good-looking" and visionary young men became in the West, "mirrors" of Christ, while certain women, favored by the painters there, became models for the form of the Theotokos. In other words, this or that sensually beautiful woman presented her form to many painters for the representation of the immaculate and All-holy Theotokos! Thusly, Filippo Lippi (1406-1469) used his lover and finally wife, Lucrezia Buti, as the model for the Virgin Mary.[78] She was the model for the Virgin in a large number of pictures, of which we mention those

---

[77] According to Theodotos, bishop of Ancyra (5th cent.), Martin Jugie, *Patrologia Orientalis*, XIX, 3, II *Homélies Mariales Byzantines* (Paris, 1925), pp. 212 f.
[78] See J. B. Supino, *Les deux Lippi* (French translation, 1904).

found in the Uffici of Florence: "The Virgin and Child," "The Virgin kneeling before the Child," "The Virgin worshipping the Child," "The Birth of Jesus Christ," "The crowning of the Virgin,"[79] and "The child-holding Virgin" found in the Pitti Palace of the same city.[80] Likewise, the famous Raphael (1483-1520)[81] used as his model for the Virgin Mary his much beloved flower-girl of Florence. This particular model we recognize, among others, in the picture kept at the above mentioned Pitti Palace and called "The Virgin of the Grand Duke,"[82] in "The Holy Family" of the Museum Louvre, a picture called "Francisco I,"[83] in the Virgin of the same Museum named "The Beautiful Gardener,"[84] and others. Also, Fornarina, who is exalted in poems by Raphael and whom we find in the canvas "La Dame au Voile"[85] of the Pitti Palace, is the same model we encounter as the child-holding Virgin in Dresden, also known as the Sistine Madonna.[86] Rubens again (1577-1640) had for a model of the Virgin his friend and later second wife, Helen Fourment, whom we find pictured in a large canvas, "The Birth of Christ," in the Haus der Kunst of Munich, in "The Holy Family" of the Pitti Palace,[87] and others. Especially characteristic is the picture of St. George found in the chapel of the painter's tomb, in which Rubens has depicted holy persons with the figures of his family, while with his own image he has represented St. George! Titian (1477-1576) also did not hesitate to present Eleonora Gonzaga as a completely nude "Reclining Aphrodite,"[88] as shown in the canvas of the Museum of Dresden, and later as the "Virgin with the child Jesus," a picture which we find in the Uffici of Florence.[89] Moreover, we know that Agnès Sorel agreed to model, for example, for Jean Fouquet, as the "Nursing Virgin Mary,"

---

[79] See J. Fattorusso, *Florence* (Florence, 1952), pp. 124, 125.

[80] *Ibid.*, p. 177

[81] E. Müntz, *Raphaël, sa vie, son oeuvre, et son temps* (Paris, 1899) and A. Rosenbberg et Gronau, *Rafael*, 4th edition (Stuttgart, 1909).

[82] J. Mesnil, *Raphael, coll. des maîtres*, illustration 18.

[83] Hachette, *Les plus beaux tableaux du Louvre*, illustration 22.

[84] *Ibid..* illustration 23.

[85] Flattorusso, *ibid.*, p. 163.

[86] Galerie royal, 1516.

[87] Mesnil, *ibid.*, illustration 54.

[88] Fattorusso, *op. cit.*, illustration 162.

[89] *Ibid.*, p. 142.

but on the inviolable condition that her breasts be shown completely naked and especially that the nipples be emphasized. The picture of this painter (15th century) in the Museum of Antwerp is just another example.[90]

Many of these Virgins of Western painters and similar copper engravings were widely circulated in the Orthodox world from the Turkish domination and after. From the lithographies later (from the 19th century) came copies of oil-paintings which we find in Orthodox churches. But even when these western types were not copied completely, they, nevertheless, influenced Orthodox iconography most significantly through their sentimentally appealing "sweet" forms. Thus, becoming popular among our people, these icons served only to idealize the erotic passion of the painters and to perpetuate their sentimental emotions, which are, however, entirely unrelated to the holy emotion demanded of the icon by the tradition of strict Orthodoxy. Such icons of the Theotokos which recall to mind, for example, Fornarina of Raphael or copy portraits of other women (we are not speaking, certainly, of those situations in which by the same model even the nude Aphrodite was pictured!) are strictly unacceptable to Orthodoxy. Also, it must be noted here that the Ρ' (100) Canon of the Sixth Ecumenical Council clearly condemned such form of Iconography as kindling the sensual mind: τὰς οὖν τὴν ὅρασιν καταγοητευούσας γραφάς, εἴτε ἐν πίναξιν, εἴτε ἄλλως πως ἀνατιθεμένας καὶ τὸν νοῦν διαφθειρούσας καὶ κινούσας πρὸς τὰς τῶν αἰσχρῶν ἡδονῶν ὑπεκαύσεις, οὐδαμῶς ἀπὸ τοῦ νῦν, οἵωδήποτε τρόπῳ, προστάττομεν ἐγχαράττεσθαι. (Those paintings, therefore, be they on panels or any other place, which fascinate the vision and corrupt the mind and incite the fires of shameful pleasures, we command that in no wise from now on and in no manner whatsoever be they engraved.)[91]

From all that we have said above, one should not think that Orthodox iconography, during its long process, ignored the natural reality, that is, the so-called realistic element. Of course, as an art essentially spiritual and concerned for the expression of

---

[90] See I. Reau, Παγκόσμια Ἱστορία τῆς Τέχνης (World History of Art), Greek trans. by K. Pangalos (Athens, 1955), vol. 1, p. 539.

[91] See Πηδάλιον, Edition by Astir (Athens, 1957), p. 310. (Pedalion —Rudder: a collection of Church Canons.)

the spiritual world, it insisted — especially during its formative centuries — on making its true character understood. But, as we have seen from the representation of the Crucifixion (the Theotokos standing before the Cross, etc.) and shall see more in the following chapter, Byzantine painting did not ignore the realistic element especially from the period of the Palaeologoi. This element of realism, however, was not used as in the West, nor even as we perhaps understand it today (being taught so by the Renaissance), but rather for a definite purpose and only after it was subordinated and assimilated to the whole vigorous spiritual power of Byzantine art. Whereas in the Western art the element of realism constituted an end in itself, that is, it was sought as an artistic ideal, [92] in Orthodox art, on the contrary, it served another purpose, that is, *the necessity to subordinate the material element to the spiritual,* our lower nature to our higher — a thing which is manifest and expressed by the complete subordination of the realistic element to the higher spirituality achieved in the creations of this art. Moreover, the manifest subordination of the material to the spiritual in these icons shows also the beauty of high quality which the first element comes to possess from the second, that is the beauty which the material element ἐνδύεται ("puts on") when it is dominated by the life-giving and life-transforming power of the spirit of Christ.[93] Christ, μορφωθεὶς τὸ καθ' ἡμᾶς, ἐθέωσε τὸ πρόσλημμα (being formed in likeness to us, deified what He received).[94] And it is this deification, this *theosis* of the human nature that is made perceptible by this form of Orthodox iconography.

---

[92] It has been correctly noted that the works of Rubens purpose to show τὴν φρικίασιν τῆς ἡδυπαθείας (the shudder of voluptuousness) or better τὴν φρικίασιν τῆς ὀργώσης σαρκὸς (the horror of the lusting flesh), I. M. Panayiotopoulos, in the *Great Greek Encyclopedia,* vol. 21, p. 263.

[93] In regard to the "formation" of Christ in us, as St. Paul writes: μέχρις οὗ μορφωθῇ Χριστὸς ἐν ὑμῖν (until Christ be formed in you), Gal. 4:19.

[94] *Menaion* of December 24, p. 183. Cf. P. N. Trembelas, 'Εκλογὴ 'Ορθοδόξου 'Υμνογραφίας [Selection of Orthodox Hymns] (Athens, 1949), p. 135. Cf. also the Akathistos Hymn . . . δι' ἧς (Θεοτόκου) ἡμεῖς ἐθεώθημεν (by whom — the Theotokos — we were deified), *The Great Horologion,* ed. Saliverou, p. 531.

CHAPTER TWO

THE FORM OF ORTHODOX ICONOGRAPHY

«Ὁ ἀπερίγραπτος Λόγος τοῦ Πατρός . . . περιεγράφη σαρκούμενος, καὶ τὴν ρυπωθεῖσαν εἰκόνα εἰς τὸ ἀρχαῖον ἀναμορφώσας τῷ θείῳ κάλλει συγκατέμιξεν».

"The uncircumscribed Logos of the Father was circumscribed by becoming incarnate, and by transforming the darkened image to the original, united it with the divine beauty."

(Kontakion of Sunday of Orthodoxy)

The particular form of Orthodox iconography is especially interesting not only in itself, but also for the whole understanding of this art's content. Matter and form, that is, content and style are here in such relationship that the one interprets the other and both together interpret the real essence of Orthodox iconography. The research into this form, therefore, is a very important subject; its ignorance during the past centuries has led to misinterpretation and to its neglect by many. A consequence of this neglect is undoubtedly the lack of emphasis in contemporary Orthodox worship of the primarily liturgical significance of this art. This means the deprivation of worship of a fundamental element, an element especially contributive to the expression of its strong power and its incomparable spiritual superiority — as indicated by its long tradition.

Before we proceed to the examination of the particular elements constituting this form of iconography, it is necessary to see the more general presuppositions which led to it.

A. MORE GENERAL PRESUPPOSITIONS OF FORM IN ORTHODOX ICONOGRAPHY

The knowledge of the reasons dictating the particular form which Orthodox iconography utilized is necessary precisely because it is such ignorance which often compares the form of this art with the religious art of the West and, as a result, condemns the Byzantine form as being erroneous, primitive, unnatural, and other such things. Western art is admired for rendering the power of naturalism, for presenting real physiognomies and environment, while Byzantine art is criticized for its weakness in rendering natural reality, natural beauty, grace and variety. But it is precisely in this negative verification that the value of Byzantine art lies,

44

and it is this point which concerns its entire particular form.

We have already seen that the content of Orthodox iconography became the καινὴ κτίσις ("new creation") in Christ. The high theology of this new creation in Christ and the actual life-experience in worship of its revelation concentrated the entire interest of this art. The common world, the world of decay was wholly unrelated to it. The ρυπωθεῖσα εἰκὼν (darkened or unclean image) of the world and of man, which resulted from the πτῶσις (the fall),[1] was contrasted by the Church to the image of the world[2] and of man which was renewed by the ὑπερπερισσεύσασαν (over-abundant) Grace.[3] In order, therefore, for Orthodox art to be able to express this work of Grace, which the Church proclaims, it was necessary that even its form be analogous. For this reason, the iconographies which aimed at expressing the holiness of the persons could not have been mere portraits, that is, pictures which direct us to natural people. Rather they had to be creations of a particular morphological conception which dismiss the spectator from the transience of this world and impose upon him the idea of the reborn creation, of the eternal world, of the Kingdom of God.

A basic presupposition of the form, therefore, was this idea of a "new" man and world in Christ. The Sacred Scripture, the Fathers of the Church and the Ecumenical Councils formulated and developed this idea and presented it to the Church. The art was obligated from the beginning to follow and to μορφώσῃ (formulate, fashion)[4] this idea, that is, this fundamental belief of the Church. Thus, the art form was subordinated to the authority of the Church;[5] it became its property and only the technical part

---

[1] Οἴδαμεν γὰρ ὅτι πᾶσα ἡ κτίσις συστενάζει καὶ συνωδίνει ἄχρι τοῦ νῦν (for we know that all creation bemoans and travails together (with man) until now), Rom. 8:22.

[2] Ὅτι καὶ αὐτὴ ἡ κτίσις ἐλευθερωθήσεται ἀπὸ τῆς δουλείας τῆς φθορᾶς (for that creation also will be liberated from the bondage of corruption . . .), Rom. 8:21.

[3] Rom. 5:20.

[4] Regarding this "morphosis" in the ecclesiastical sense and the recent movement to promote it, see the exceptional and fully informative studies of Evangelos Theodorou, Ἡ Λειτουργικὴ Μόρφωσις καὶ Ἀγωγὴ (The Liturgical Instruction and Education), Athens, 1958, p. 11 f., and Ἡ Μορφωτικὴ Ἀξία τοῦ Ἰσχύοντος Τριῳδίου (The Instructive Value of the Triodeon in Use). Athens, 1958, pp. 69 f.

[5] Cf. also A. Grabar (Skira), *La peinture byzantine*, p. 34.

was made the concern of the iconographers.[6] The Seventh Ecumenical Council decided that τῶν ζωγράφων ἐφεύρεσις ἡ τῶν εἰκόνων ποίησις, ἀλλὰ τῆς καθολικῆς ἐκκλησίας ἔγκριτος θεσμοθεσία καὶ παράδοσις, τοῦ ζωγράφου ἡ τέχνη μόνον, ἡ δὲ διάταξις τῶν δειμαμένων ἁγίων πατέρων. (the invention of the painters is the icon's creation, but the distinguished institution and tradition belongs to the catholic Church. For to the painter belongs the art only, while the order of fundamentals belongs to the holy Fathers).[7] By contrast, in the West, from the council of Frankfurt (794), no dogmatic-theological or liturgical significance was attributed to art; it was regarded simply as an element "for the decoration of the churches."[7a] This is the reason why it was left free and uncontrolled in the hands, the subjective ideas and the mentality of irresponsible painters.

Orthodox iconography, however, directed and guarded by the Church, gave the appropriate form to its creed. According to the Church, the form of Christ was not to be represented as any natural man's. If Christ were pictured as an ordinary mature man (as is done in the West), it would infer the idea of His one nature, the human only; this would be a kind of nestorianism and as such dangerous to Orthodoxy. Christ, however, is God-Man, διπλοῦς τὴν φύσιν (double in nature). Now, art had to find some form, some iconographic type which would lead the spectator directly to the thought that in the represented person κατοικεῖ πᾶν τὸ πλήρωμα τῆς θεότητος σωματικῶς, (the whole fullness of the divinity dwells bodily).[8] Moreover, according to Theodore Studites, ἄν τε φαίημεν τὸν Χριστὸν Θεοῦ δύναμιν καὶ Θεοῦ σοφίαν, ὡσαύτως καὶ τὸ αὐτοῦ ἀπεικόνισμα Θεοῦ δύναμις καὶ Θεοῦ σοφία εἴρηται, (if we say that Christ is the power of God and the wisdom of God, by the same manner His representation must be said to be the power and the wisdom of God.)[8a] This presupposition directed the inspiration of the Orthodox iconographers to that morpho-

---

[6] See also *Encyclopédie Populaire des Connaissances Liturgiques* (Paris, Bloud et Gay, 1947, pp. 213 f.

[7] Mansi, *Sacr. Cons. nova et empl. collectio,* XIII, p. 252.

[7a] See Ch. J. Héfélé, *Histoire des Conciles,* III 2 (Paris, 1907-10), pp. 1067 f.

[8] Collosians 2:9, But which Western picture of the Lord imposes the idea that in the represented Christ the whole fullnesss of divinity dwells bodily?

[8a] Migne, P.G. 99, 361.

logically ideal type, by which — as far as it is possible to art — they represented the *Person* of the Lord Jesus Christ, of God the Logos, granted that in His person the two natures are united without confusion and change. The humanly "beautiful" Christs of Western art, or those purely human types influenced by them, are dogmatically reprehensible and, therefore, unacceptable for us since they denote the idea of only the human nature of the Lord. The decision of the Seventh Ecumenical Council stated that the Church, even though she may depict the Lord through art in His human form, does not separate in the representation Christ's flesh from His divinity, since it is united in Him and, is ὁμόθεος καὶ ὁμότιμος (co-divine and of equal honor).[9] Christ is, therefore, represented in Orthodox art as *God-Man* (theanthropos), the divinity being alluded to in the representation of His holy Body (which is always referred to the hypostatic union of the two natures); this again is indicated by the hymn-writer who, being filled with much adoration (from the idea of divinity that such an icon denotes), writes the following: Ποίοις οἱ γηγενεῖς ὄμμασιν, ἐποψώμεθά σου τὴν εἰκόνα; ἣν τὰ τῶν ἀγγέλων στρατεύματα βλέπειν ἀδεῶς οὐ δεδύνηται, θεϊκῷ φωτὶ ἀστραπτομένην . . . (With what eyes shall we creatures of earth see thine image? The image which the armies of angels cannot see without fear as it shines in divine light?)[10]

Of course, Christ as God, as the ἀπερίγραπτος Λόγος τοῦ Πατρὸς (the uncircumscribed Logos of the Father) is even for art ἀπαράστατος (unrepresentable). Moreover, Θεὸν οὐδεὶς ἑώρακε

---

[9] Mansi, *Sacr. Cons. nova et ampl. collectio* XIII, 344. For the ὁμόθεον καὶ ὁμότιμον τοῦ Χριστοῦ σάρκα (co-divine and co-honorable body of Christ) see also the synodical Letter for Orthodoxy of the Seventh Ecumenical Council, in *Triodeon*, ed. Apostolici Diaconia of the Church of Greece, Athens, 1960, p. 147. See also p. 148: Τῶν λεγόντων ὅτι ἡ σὰρξ τοῦ Κυρίου ἐξ αὐτῆς ἑνώσεως ὑπερυψωθεῖσα καὶ ἀνωτάτω πάσης τιμῆς ὑπερκειμένη, ἐξ ἄκρας ἑνώσεως ὁμόθεος γενομένη, ἀμεταβλήτως . . . ἀναλλοιώτως μένουσα τῷ προσλαμβανομένῳ αὐτὴν Θεῷ Λόγῳ . . . αἰωνία ἡ μνήμη, (May the memory be eternal of those who say that the flesh of Christ was over-exalted by its union and is found beyond the highest honor, being equally divine by utter union, and remaining immutably and invariably with the Divine Logos who received it). Also, according to Theodore Studites: ἐμίχθη τὰ ἄμικτα, ἐν τῷ ἀπεριγράπτῳ τὸ περιγραμμένον, (the unmixable were mingled; in the uninscribable, the inscribed), Migne, P.G. 99, 409 C.

[10] *Menaion,* August 16 (In the Psalm "Lord I cry unto Thee").

πώποτε (no one has ever seen God) (John 1:18). But once the Son καὶ Σωτὴρ ἡμῶν Ἰησοῦς Χριστὸς (and Saviour Jesus Christ) (Titus 2:13), ὁ ὢν ἐπὶ πάντων Θεὸς (who is God over all . . .) (Rom. 9:5), ἄσαρκος ὢν ἐσαρκώθη ἑκών, καὶ γέγονεν ὃ οὐκ ἦν δι' ἡμᾶς (was willingly incarnated, being unincarnate, and became what he was not, for us), that is, He μετέσχε τοῦ ἡμετέρου φυράματος, (partook of our nature)[12] by utter condescension, He *became circumscribable* and therefore necessarily representable. With the reception of the flesh προσέλαβε καὶ τὰ ἰδιώματα αὐτῆς ἅπαντα (He also received all of its attributes) in which, of course, the circumscribable is founded.[13] Theodore Studites noted also: ἐσχηματίσθη ὁ ἀσχημάτιστος· καὶ ὁ ἄποσος εἴσω ποσότητος ἐγεγόνει, (the unformed received form, and the one of no quantity has become equal to quantity).[14] Since, therefore, ἑαυτὸν ὁ ἀόρατος ὁρατὸν παρεσκεύασεν, (the invisible one made himself visible)[15] through the incarnation and thusly ἑωράκαμεν τοῖς ὀφθαλμοῖς ἡμῶν (we have seen with our eyes) His face and ἐθεασάμεθα καὶ αἱ χεῖρες ἡμῶν ἐψηλάφησαν (we have seen and our hands have touched),[16] we became, consequently, capable of τὸ εἶδος τὸ τῆς ἐμφερείας αὐτοῦ ἐγγράφειν, (inscribing the form of His resemblance).[17] For this reason,

---

[11] *Triodeon, op. cit.,* p. 137.

[12] *Menaion,* December 25 (ed. Venice, 1890), p. 197.

[13] *Triodeon,* p. 134: Φύσει ἀπερίγραπτος, τῇ θεϊκῇ σου ὑπάρχων, ἐπ' ἐσχάτων Δέσποτα σαρκωθεὶς ἠξίωσας περιγράφεσθαι, (Being in Thy divine nature indescribable Lord, in these last days Thou made it possible to be circumscribed by becoming incarnate).

[14] Migne, P.G. 99, 413 C.

[15] E. Schwarz, *Acta concil. oecum. consil. univers. Chalcedonese,* I, 1, p. 13.

[16] I John 1:1-2.

[17] *Triodeon,* p. 134. Cf. also the hymn: Ὁ ἄνω τοῖς Χερουβὶμ ὢν ἀθεώρητος ὁρᾶται διὰ γραφῆς οἷσπερ ὁμοίωται . . . (He who is above unobserved by the Cherubim is seen by representation of those to whom He was assimilated) (*Menaion,* August 16). Moreover, in agreement with the words of Christ: ὁ ἑωρακὼς ἐμὲ ἑώρακε τὸν Πατέρα (he who has seen me has seen the Father) (John 14:9); ἐγὼ καὶ ὁ Πατὴρ ἕν ἐσμεν (I and the Father are one), and with the teaching of the Church about the son as ὁμοούσιος τῷ Πατρὶ (consubstantial with the Father) etc., it is necessary to note also God the Father in the icons of the Son in Orthodox iconography, such as, for example, the type of the Pantocrator. And this is especially true since each person of the tri-hypostatic and indivisible Divinity (and in this case the Son) is at the same time the bearer of the divine essence and power and also the whole God. Cf. Ch. Androutsos,

since then, the Orthodox Ἐκκλησία, τὴν ἔνσωμον εἰκόνα τοῦ Χριστοῦ ὡς ὑπερκόσμιον κόσμον ἐπαμφιέννυται, (Church is redecorated in the bodily icon of Christ which is as a beauty beyond this world),[18] and through which her iconography seeks the μόρφωσιν τῆς σαρκώσεως τοῦ Δεσπότου τῶν ὅλων, τῶν παθημάτων, (representation of the incarnation of the Lord of all, of His sufferings),[19] and of the other events of His life.

These dogmatic presuppositions of the form of iconography (which the West never took into account) are extended certainly to the person of the Theotokos and to the Saints. Orthodox iconography formulated the icon of the Mother of God by an iconographic type which does not depict her as a woman of a usually normal naturalistic form, but rather indicates her *all-holiness* and leads one to the great Mystery which was accomplished through her. According to Patriarch Germanos: Τῆς κατὰ σάρκα ἀχράντου αὐτοῦ (τοῦ Χριστοῦ) Μητρός, τῆς ἁγίας Θεοτόκου . . . τὴν ὁμοί-

---

Δογματικὴ (Dogmatics), pp. 39-92. See also John Damascene, *First Oration about Icons*, Migne, P.G. 94, 1240: εἰκὼν τοίνυν ζῶσα, φυσικὴ καὶ ἀπαράλλακτος τοῦ ἀοράτου Θεοῦ, ὁ Υἱός, ὅλον ἐν ἑαυτῷ φέρων τὸν Πατέρα, κατὰ πάντα ἔχων τὴν πρὸς αὐτὸν ταυτότητα, (therefore, a living image, natural and unchangeable of the invisible God is the Son, bearing in himself the whole Father and possessing in everything identity with Him). But the representation of God the Father (especially together with the other two Persons of the Holy Trinity) began to be known in Byzantine art from the 11th century. Thus, we have God the Father, but as the παλαιὸν τῶν ἡμερῶν (the ancient-one of days) in a wall-painting of San Biagio in Brindisi, and in the codex Paris. gr. 1208 of the National Library in Paris, dated in the 12th century (Grabar, *La peinture byzantine*, p. 183). With the Son and the Holy Spirit (Holy Trinity) we have Him in the codex Suppl. gr. 22 of Vienna (see Gestinger, *Die griechische Buchmalerei*, Wien, 1926, p. 34, illustr. XVIII). In the 13th century we find Him in the same representation of the codex 524 in the Library of San Marco of Venice (see *New Hellenomnymon*, p. 6). In the 14th century we find Him in the Psalter of Munich (see edition of Strzygowski, illustr. XXXVII) and later in the wall-paintings and the panel icons. Thus, in the beginning, God the Father appeared as the "Ancient of Days" (Daniel 7:9) and after, He was represented together with the two other Persons of the Holy Trinity by a personification in an icon of the Holy Trinity, which became popular from the 14th century. (About the old type of the Holy Trinity in the representation of the Hospitality of Abraham see my study *The Byzantine Wall-paintings of Crete*, p. 96.

[18] *Triodeon*, (Glory Hymn: "The Grace has shown . . ."), p. 134.

[19] *Ibid.*, p. 142.

ωσιν ἀνιστοροῦμεν, δεικνύοντες ὅτι τὸν Θεὸν τὸν ἀόρατον καὶ τὰ πάντα τῇ χειρὶ περιέποντα ἐν τῇ ἑαυτῆς συνέλαβε γαστρὶ καὶ ἐξ αὐτῆς σαρκω-θέντα ἀπεκύησε, (We picture the likeness of His (Christ's) pure Mother according to the flesh, the holy Theotokos . . . by indicating (that is, by the form of this iconography) that she conceived in her womb the invisible God who tends diligently to all things with His hand, and who, being made incarnate by her, was brought forth). [20] Therefore, by the "form" of the Theotokos the Ortho-dox iconography seeks to indicate directly the dogma of the In-carnation and not simply to present to us the simple virgin of Nazareth before the Πνεῦμα Ἅγιον καὶ δύναμις Ὑψίστου (Holy Spirit and power from the Highest) came to overshadow her[21] and thus to make her *the Virgin* and *truly the Mother of God.* Unfortunately, the painters of the Virgin in the West persisted in a virgin of Nazareth before the Grace.[22] Thus, Roman Catho-lics continue even today to portray her as such, even though one would expect that their recent dogma (1854) of the Immaculate Conception would influence them to formulate a more spiritual type for the Virgin Mary.[23]

The teaching of the Church appears most creative also in the entire formation of the iconographic types of the Saints. The Saints and Martyrs lived the "new" life in Christ, they struggled in the present life, and achieved the ἄφθαρτον στέφος (incor-ruptible crown) of the heavenly life. Each one of them became a type of the regeneration in Christ, an icon which Christ εἰς τὸ ἀρχαῖον ἀναμορφώσας τῷ θείῳ κάλλει συγκατέμιξεν, (reformed to the original by uniting it with the divine beauty).[24] Their represented figures, therefore, could not have been the material and corruptible (those before grace), but those of ἁγιότητος (holiness), that is,

---

[20] Migne, P.G. 98, 157 C. But what western icon of the Theotokos proves by its form the great Mystery of the Incarnation of God the Logos, which was accomplished by the Mother of God?

[21] Luke 1:35.

[22] The proclamation of the Virgin Mary begins with the verification of the angel that she has found "grace in the sight of God." Luke 1:31.

[23] For details regarding the error of this dogma see J. O. Kalogerou, Μαρία ἡ Ἀειπάρθενος Θεοτόκος κατὰ τὴν Ὀρθόδοξον Πίστιν (Mary the Ever-Virgin Theotokos according to the Orthodox Faith), Salonika, 1957, pp. 81 f.

[24] *Triodeon,* p. 137.

those of heavenly δόξης (glory), with which they were clothed.[25] Here again, therefore, Orthodox iconography moves from the belief of the Church that ἑτέρα μὲν ἡ τῶν ἐπουρανίων (σωμάτων) δόξα, ἑτέρα δὲ ἡ τῶν ἐπιγείων, (one is the glory of the heavenly (bodies), and another of the earthly).[26] The saints and the martyrs are regarded as ἐπουράνιοι (heavenly), citizens of heaven. And because οἷος ὁ ἐπουράνιος τοιοῦτοι καὶ οἱ ἐπουράνιοι (as the heavenly one is, so also are they who are heavenly),[27] the saints are represented with such a schematic composition in order to dismiss one directly from the forms of daily life, that is, the forms of corruption and to inspire the blessed reality beyond this world, where the light of the Incorruptible and heavenly God shines. The physiognomies of the saints, therefore, as they are rendered in the wall-paintings and in the portable icons of our Church, become a continual commentary to the faithful that δεῖ τὸ φθαρτὸν ἐνδύσασθαι ἀφθαρσίαν καὶ τὸ θνητὸν ἐνδύσασθαι ἀθανασίαν, (the corruptible must be clothed in incorruptibility and the mortal in immortality).[28] In other words, Orthodox iconography attempts here to give, in some manner, an idea of the spiritual bodies which will follow the resurrection of the dead, to express the ἑτέραν δόξαν τῶν ἐπουρανίων καὶ ἐν ἀφθαρσίᾳ σωμάτων, (other glory of the heavenly and incorruptible bodies).[29]

B. More Particular Elements of Form in Orthodox Iconography

1. *The Sacred Physiognomies*

After the quick exposition of the more general reasons for the form of Orthodox iconography, we proceed now, specifically, to the examination of its more particular elements.

---

[25] Cf. the often repeated phrase in the dismissal hymns of the Church regarding the saints: δόξα τῷ σὲ δοξάσαντι Χριστῷ . . . (glory to Christ who glorified thee . . .).

[26] I Cor. 15:40.

[27] I Cor. 15:48.

[28] I Cor. 15:53. Also, καθὼς ἐφορέσαμεν τὴν εἰκόνα τοῦ χοϊκοῦ, φορέσομεν καὶ τὴν εἰκόνα τοῦ ἐπουρανίου, (As we have borne the image of the earthly, we shall also bear the image of the heavenly).

[29] I Cor. 15:40, 48. Cf. also Philippians 3:21: ὃς μετασχηματίσει τὸ σῶμα τῆς ταπεινώσεως ἡμῶν, εἰς τὸ γενέσθαι αὐτὸ σύμμορφον τῆς δόξης αὐτοῦ, (who shall change our body of humility to become fashioned like (the body of) His glory).

First of all, the sacred physiognomies manifest technically the faces and their naked parts in a manner absolutely in agreement with whatever was said above. The iconographer, with a few colors, with full but steady and vital use of the brush, renders the spirit of his sublime art. In the art of the catacombs[30] and in the miniatures,[31] the artist, with a minimum of "brush strokes," deliniates the facial characteristics in their simplest form. The same is true with the wall-paintings. For example, in the famous Divine Liturgy of the Perivleptos church of Mystra,[32] with a few white lights upon the prominent parts (forehead, nose, cheeks, beard) of the face, whose general tone (προπλασμὸς) is of deep chestnut-color, the unknown artist succeeded in creating supraworldly forms, shadows and visions from another world. Two white dots on each side of the nose become capable of indicating (in the midst of the whole shadowy face) the glow of the world of God as well as the τρόμος καὶ φόβος (fear and trembling) of heavenly Powers serving the great Mystery.

The general procedure for the depiction of the faces consists in drawing the features with gray or black pigment into a middle tone painted either with yellow ocher, or with a warmer ocher mixed with red.[33] The same pigment of gray or black is used for painting the outlines which separate the faces from the background and at the same time enhance their vitality. At times in the wall paintings, but more often in the portable icons dating from the 16th century, the general color tone of the faces and also of the nude areas of the bodies is painted dark or chestnut-colored. Over this tone are painted a few lights shaped either as spots, or as very thin parallel whitish lines, referred to as ψιμμυθιαί. The latter are painted either directly over the dark ground, creat-

---

[30] See examples in the recent edition of W. F. Volbach and M. Hirmer, *Frühchristliche Kunst, Die Kunst der spätantike in West und Ostrom,* München, 1958, p. 7 (from the catacomb of SS. Callistus and Domitilla), p. 9 (catacomb of SS. Callistus and Priscilla), p. 10 (St. Domitilla).

[31] As an example see the codex of Rossano (6th century). A good picture of its pages see in Grabar, *Peinture Byzantine,* pp. 162, 163.

[32] Regarding the liturgical significance of this wall-painting, we have already spoken above, p. 16 f.

[33] Often we have the characteristic wheat-colored base as for example in the Ὄμορφη Ἐκκλησιὰ of Patesia, Athens.

ing an effect of abrupt transition from the shaded area to the light; or they are painted in several color gradations, successively toned downward: a process known as γλυκασμός.

This use of outlines is an integral part of the calligraphic manner or technique of painting, whereby the element of line is employed for depicting the features and details of the faces (plates 2, 3). The use of chiaroscuro, on the other hand, is either minimal, or totally absent. Nevertheless, Orthodox hagiography is not entirely oblivious to the opposite or impressionistic technique of painting whereby all outlines or hard contours are avoided, and other linear elements are either limited or totally absent, and chiaroscuro becomes dominant, enhancing the mass as well as the details[34] (plates 13, 18, 19, 20, 22).

The same principles govern the *style* of our iconography in the formation of the details in the sacred physiognomies. That is to say, the eyes, the nose, the ears (the sensory organs) are not rendered according to nature, to the anatomical truth, because each of them, having sensed and received the divine Revelation, has become now an organ of the spirit and "has been changed" (ἠλλοι-ώθη). This change of every sensory organ is interpreted by Orthodox iconography, especially by the known *styl.zation.* By means of the so often misinterpreted schematic order, this sublime art attempts to denote that each sensory organ, having received the divine Grace and having contributed in its appropriation by the represented sacred person, was sanctified and therefore has ceased to be the usual sensory organ of the biological man. Thus, we can understand why, at first, the eyes are painted large and animated[35] (plate 2), expressive of physical intensity. Because they have seen the great things, they have been opened to the sublime[36] and, of course, through them the study of the divine Law and the vision of the works of the Creator have entered into the conscience of the represented saint. Through those large eyes the represented

---

[34] See examples in Grabar, *Peinture Byzantine, op. cit.,* pp. 166, 168, 171, 173.

[35] See e.g. the sacred faces in the mosaics of Hosios Loukas near Levadeia, Diez-Demus, *Byzantine Mosaics in Greece; Hosios Lucas,* 1931.

[36] Cf. Psalm 118:18 (119): 'Αποκάλυψον τοὺς ὀφθαλμούς μου καὶ κατανοήσω τὰ θαυμάσια ἐκ τοῦ νόμου σου, (Open Thou mine eyes that I may behold wondrous things out of Thy law).

53

saints verify: Οἱ ὀφθαλμοί μου διαπαντὸς πρὸς τὸν Κύριον. Εἶδον οἱ ὀφθαλμοί μου τὸ σωτήριόν σου . . . Ἐμελέτησα ἐν πᾶσι τοῖς ἔργοις σου, ἐν ποιήμασι τῶν χειρῶν σου ἐμελέτησα, (Mine eyes are ever toward the Lord; for mine eyes have seen Thy salvation . . . I meditate on all Thy works, on the creation of Thy hands have I mused).[37] Likewise we can understand why the ears are drawn large (usually characteristically stylized).[38] They have been widened to hear the commandments of the Lord, and through them the saint εἰσακήκοε τῆς θείας οἰκονομίας τὸ μυστήριον (has heard the mystery of divine economy). They are rather in a symbolic sense a projection of the ears of the soul, which ἐγένοντο προσέχοντα (became attentive) since those of nature have been shut to the noise τοῦ αἰῶνος τούτου (of this world). The nose also is often larger than its natural length and thin (plates 18, 19), because it is not meant to perform a physiological service, that is, it does not smell the things of this world, but the ὀσμὴν εὐωδίας πνευματικῆς (smell of spiritual fragrance), the εὐωδίαν τῆς Ἁγίας Τριάδος (the fragrance of the Holy Trinity), according to Didymus the Blind,[39] or the ὀσμὴν τῆς ἀφθαρσίας (smell of incorruption) which Christ and the Holy Spirit emit, according to Irenaeus.[40]

The same things are true even for the mouth. The mouth is shaped small to denote by that, that the represented sacred person, obeying the commandment μὴ μεριμνᾶτε τῇ ψυχῇ ὑμῶν τί φάγητε ἢ τί πίητε, (take no thought for your life, what ye shall eat, or what ye shall drink),[41] limited himself to the indispensable and necessary food for preservation; seeking πρῶτον τὴν βασιλείαν τοῦ Θεοῦ καὶ τὴν δικαιοσύνην αὐτοῦ, (first the Kingdom of God and His righteousness),[42] συνεκάλυψε δὲ ἐν τῇ νηστείᾳ τὴν ψυχήν του (he has chastened his soul with fasting).[43] Moreover, the small mouth is

---

[37] Psalm 24:15 (25); St. Luke 2:30; Psalm 142:5 (143).

[38] The stylization is also common in the hair and the beard. Iconography often renders the curled hair with well arranged small rounded bodies or twisted folds, or with wave-like, uniformly successive curves; the beard is shaped in the same manner. All these denote the willful avoidance of representing the natural man in favor of manifesting the "other glory" of the spiritual man.

[39] Migne, P.G. 39, 589.

[40] Ibid, 7, 480.

[41] St. Matthew 6:25.

[42] Ibid., 6:38.

[43] Psalm 68:11 (69:10).

also a more general indication of spirituality, a symbolism of the paradisiacal blessedness of a body materially not in need, a body which, according to Cyril of Jerusalem, οὐκέτι τροφῶν τοιούτων χρείαν ἔχει πρὸς ζωήν . . . γίνεται γὰρ πνευματικὸν θαυμάσιόν τι καὶ οἷον εἰπεῖν κατ' ἀξίαν οὐκ ἔχομεν, (no longer has need of such foods for sustaining life . . . for it becomes a spiritual wonder of which we cannot speak worthily).[44]

The heads of the saints are encircled in the known crown of light (nimbus, halo). Many have the impression that its use (together with certain other points) is enough to denote the "holiness" of the represented person. This has been taught by the religious art of the West, whose sacred persons are so worldly in appearance that the nimbus is indispensable to signify that a saint is being represented. In Orthodox art, however, one does not depend upon the crown of light alone to understand that the represented person is a saint. Holiness is indicated by the entire form, the technic and the style of iconography. Certainly, even the crown of light is one characteristic of the holiness of the depicted physiognomies, and has with us a profounder meaning than in the West, as we shall see. But because the whole style of our iconography denotes directly the sacredness of the represented persons, we can say that the crown of light — even though it is of the elements of Orthodox art — does not have a basic significance as it is usually thought. In fact, it is missing from the iconography of older Christian representation as well as from certain scenes in the iconography of the Byzantine period. Thus, in the wall-paintings of the catacombs, Christ, the Theotokos, the martyrs are represented without nimbus.[45] Similarly, in most of the sarcophagi of the 4th century especially, and in the ivory engravings from the 4th to the 6th centuries, as well as in some mosaics, there is no crown of light.[46] In the iconographic scenes of the

---

44 Migne, P.G. 33, 613, Catechesis 18.

45 See e.g. Christ as the good Shepherd in the catacomb of St. Callistus in Rome; Christ among the twelve Apostles in the catacomb of St. Domitilla; the Theotokos and Child in the catacomb of St. Priscilla, etc. See picture in Volbach-Hirmer, op. cit., illustr. 7-10.

46 See e.g. the sarcophagus called the adelphia of the National Museum of Syracuse, Italy, where, among other things, the Adoration of the Magi and the Palm Sunday are depicted; the sarcophagus in St. Peter's in Rome of Junius Vassa where scenes from the life of Christ and the

Byzantine period, such as e.g. the Ascension, the Dormition of the Theotokos, etc.,[47] the Apostles are usually shown without this distinctive mark.[48]

The crown of light in Orthodox iconography signifies the radiating glory of the represented person.[49] It surrounds the head

---

Apostles are shown; the sarcophagus in the Museum of St. Ambrose in Milano where Christ is shown with His disciples, and others. Also among the ivory engravings see the relic-case in the Museo Civico of Brescia which depicts Jesus, His disciples and scenes from His life (miracles, Passion). See also representations on the diptych of the cathedral church of Milano (5th century) with scenes from the life of Jesus, and the known throne of Maximianus in Ravenna, etc. Among the mosaics see the saints in the dome of St. George in Salonika. Cf. also F. Gerke, *Vorkonstantinische Sarkophage*, pp. 208 f.; G. Bovini, *I sarcofagi paleocristiani*, 1949, p. 218; J. Wilpert, *I sarcofagi Cristiani I*, illustr. 13; G. Belvederi, in *Ambrosiana*, Milano, 1942, p. 177; and Vorbach-Hirmer, *op. cit.*, illustr. 85-89, 124, 125, and 230-232.

[47] Such as Palm Sunday (Βαΐων), the Nipter (Jesus washing the feet of His disciples).

[48] See e.g. the Apostles of the Koimesis in Daphni, of the Ascension in Pantanassa, and of the Koimesis in the Perivleptos of Mystra. Likewise see the Apostles of the same scene in the Sopotchani and the Gratchanitsa of Serbia. Cf. Millet, *Mistra*, illustr. 116 and 137, also Schweinfurth, *Byz. Form*, (1st edition), illustr. 34. Grabar, *Peinture byzantine, op. cit.*, pp. 148, 149. (By contrast with a crown of light see triptych of the 10th century in Brummer Gallery, ed. title *Early Christian and Byzantine Art*, (an exhibition held at the Baltimore Museum of Art), Baltimore, 1947, illllustr. XXIX, 140. Also in the post-Byzantine icons of the Koimesis we have crowns of light. See Xyngopoulos, *Catalogue, op. cit.*, (illustr. 45, A). In other scenes again of the Byzantine and post-Byzantine period, such as e.g. the Last Supper, sometimes there are crowns of light and sometimes they are missing. See for example the Last Supper in St. Mark's of Venice (Bettini, *Mosaici antichi di San Marco a Venezia*, illustr. XIV) and by contrast see the same scene in St. Nicholas Anapausa of the Meteora (1527), a work of Theophanes of Crete, following, of course, the types of the older manuscripts. (See such in Millet, *Recherches sur l'iconographie de l'Evangile*, Paris, 1916, fig. 277-279.)

[49] The crown of light was known also in pagan art; it also encircled there the head of gods or royal persons, obviously to indicate their divine origin. The head of Buddah, for example, was often encircled with the crown of light. (Many and interesting examples can be seen in the Museum Gume of Paris.) A crown of light was also borne by royal persons of Byzantine art (see off-hand as an example Justinian and Theodora in Volbach-Hirmer, *op. cit.*, illustr. 166, 167. Cf. S. Lambros, Λεύκωμα Βυζαντινῶν Αὐτοκρατόρων (Album of Byzantine Emperors) Athens, 1930.

because the head is the center of the spirit, thought and understanding. It is understood, of course, that this light, being spherical, refers to the entire head. In art, however, it is represented as a light disk, that is, as a cut-away of the light sphere.[50] The color of this disk, which is usually gold or yellow,[51] contributes in emphasizing the whole face of the saint; the crown of light becomes, in a manner, the lighted space and the direct background in which the revered head is projected and emphasized.

In the West, even the spiritual character of this symbol of iconography was misunderstood. In most instances, it received the form of a circular brim often elliptical (for perspective reasons) sketched over and beyond the head (that is, not touching the head) of the sacred persons. Thus, the crown of light appears as something entirely external, as a crown rather of an athletic victory and not as a personal reflection, as a radiance emitted from within the form of the represented saint. Works of Ghirlandajio, Botticelli, Fra Bartolomeo, Dolci, Raphael, Da Vinci, and others are some such off-hand examples.[52]

The manner of rendering the other naked parts of the body, such as the uncovered parts of the hands and the feet, is analogous to that particular manner by which the faces and their characteristics are fashioned to express the spiritual ideal in our iconography. Both the hands and the feet are often drawn indifferently to natural truth. Often the fingers of the hands are disproportionately large, while the blessing right hand receives in many in-

----

[50] It is known that the crown of light of living persons was in the shape of a rectangle. See off-hand an example in Grabar, *Peinture byzantine*, p. 50. (Here the battlements painted behind each saint play the role of the crown of light). p. 78.

[51] There are crowns of light of different colors in one scene, usually of many persons, such as the Last Supper, the Ascension, the Resurrection, the Second Coming, etc. See as examples the Resurrection (Descent into Hades) of the Nea Moné in Chios (picture in Grabar, *ibid.*, p. 112), the Adoration of the Magi in the church of the Theotokos in Cosmidium of Rome, a work of the 8th century (*ibid.*, p. 79), the Second Coming (angels escorting the enthroned Apostles) in the church of the Theotokos in Kritsa (C. Kalokyris, Ἡ Παναγία τῆς Κριτσᾶς, Herakleion, Crete, 1952, p. 243), and others.

[52] See in this relation I. Fattorusso, *Florence*, pp. 126, 160, 161. Mesnil, *Raphael*, illustr. 18, 22, 40, 53, 59. Basler, *Leonardo da Vinci*, illustr. 13, 23.

stances the dimensions of the head.[53] The large fingers, of course, are expressive of spiritual intensity. Through them the spiritual life of the sacred person is projected and interpreted. The blessing of the Lord is not a mere gesture, but an expression of the Grace which is gifted. Especially worthy of mention are certain hands of Christ in Orthodox art. Thus, in Daphni the hands of Christ are anti-realistic, but of tremendous power to agree with His very robust face as the Pantocrator. Here the phalanx bones of the fingers are clearly distinguished from each other by an angular or curved contour, and they show such a pulsation of life and superior spiritual strength that directly —after the dominating face — they draw the whole attention of the believer and contribute in making perceptible the active presence of the Allmighty God. Especially the hand with which the Pantocrator holds the Gospel, with protruding index finger, presents something exceptionally unnatural. A. Grabar thinks it is possible that the deformation of this hand resulted from the designing difficulty of the person setting the mosaic pieces in the hollow surface of the dome.[54] We think, however, that it would be possible to regard this "deformation" as purposeful, that is, as related to the intention of the artist to symbolize the significance of the Gospel borne by this hand, to express by such a hand οὐχὶ κατὰ ἄνθρωπον (not of man) that the book it bears is not a common book, but the Book *par excellence,* the "Evangelion" which οὐκ ἔστι κατὰ ἄνθρωπον (is not of man).[55] In the icon "Touch me not" (scenes from the Resurrection) by Michael Damascenos (16th century),[56] the right hand of Christ is again of extreme interest, as it is extended toward Mary Magdalene kneeling before Him and stretching her right hand toward the Lord (plates 16, 38). Although

---

[53] Grabar, *Peinture byzantine,* p. 37.

[54] Grabar, *Peinture byzantine,* p. 118.

[55] Galatians 1:11. Our opinion is supported by the fact that the example of Daphni is not an isolated one. Similar hands holding the Gospel can be seen in the Pantocrator of the Ὄμορφη Ἐκκλησιὰ of Patesia, Athens, and of the Pammakaristos Monastery of Constantinople (Fetihe Djami). A similar meaning is expressed, in many instances, with the hands of other holy persons who bear sacred objects, e.g. of the Theotokos holding the Infant Christ, of the Evangelists holding a Gospel book, etc. In these instances the fingers are not deformed, but they are disproportionately large to denote precisely the great significance of the object they hold.

[56] It is found in the metropolitan church of St. Menas in Herakleion.

these hands are closer to the natural truth because of the particular period of iconography and the general style of Damascenos,[57] they have, nevertheless, such expressive power that, as one is extended toward the other with so much spiritual nobility and grace, they leave the viewer with the impression that they speak and that they alone were enough to render the theme of the icon. From the extended hand of Christ toward Mary who is eager to adore Him, one can sense the conveyance of the pulse of the gentle word, "Touch me not," while at the same time, from the contracting hand of Mary Magdalene, one can see the direct consequent result of the divine exhortation.

The hands of the saints too are of the same style. The Forerunner, for example, pointing with his right hand to the approaching Christ coming to be baptized, has the index finger of this hand characteristically large (ἴδε ὁ ἀμνός . . . behold the lamb . . .). This obviously notes that the indicated person is great and his work is also great. He is ὁ ἀμνὸς τοῦ Θεοῦ, ὁ αἴρων τὴν ἁμαρτίαν τοῦ κόσμου, (the lamb of God who bears the sin of the world).[58] A very good sample of expression of inner life are the fingers of the hands of Joseph crossed over his chest in the panel icon of the "Adoration of the Magi" by the iconographer Tzanfournari (17th century).[59] As we have already said in another place,[60] these lighted and very large fingers, as they extend upon his shadowy chest, "actually speak and express that which possesses his heart, that is, the obedience to the angelic prediction and the appropriate awe for the new-born Child."

We have similar observations for the feet of the saints. The legs are usually exceptionally slender (plate 9), with a strong hollowness of the soles of the feet, with long toes or, sometimes, with a peculiar flat-footed formation by an intense curving of the heel to render unnaturally even the lowest section of the limbs. Of the many examples of this last form we note as characteristic the feet

---

[57] About this artist see the study of S. Bettini, *Il pittore Michele Damasceno,* etc. in Atti del Reale Inst. Veneto di Sc. Let. ed Arti, 1934-5, vol. 94, which is, however, incomplete.

[58] John 1:29.

[59] In the Museum Benaki. Ch. Xyngopoulos, *Catalogue,* p. 34, illustr. 16.

[60] In the book Ἡ Γέννησις τοῦ Χριστοῦ εἰς τὴν Βυζαντινὴν Τέχνην τῆς Ἑλλάδος (The Birth of Christ in Byzantine Art of Greece), Athens, 1956.

of St. John the Baptist in the mosaic of the Baptism of Christ in the church of San Marco in Venice (11th century),[61] the feet of the Apostles in the representation of the Holy Communion in the church of Sopotchani in Serbia (1265) and in the scene of the Death of the Theotokos in the same church (especially the Apostles Peter and Paul),[62] of the Apostles of the Ascension in the church of Pantanassa in Mystra (15th century),[63] of Jesus in the wall-painting of the raising of Lazarus in the church of the Theotokos in Lampiotes, Crete (15th century),[64] and of others which lead us to the art of the manuscripts.[65]

Besides the faces, the hands and the feet, there are other instances where Orthodox iconography presents the bodies naked in part or in whole. This happens, for example, in the Baptism of Christ where He is depicted entirely naked or with a waist-cloth, in the Whipping and in the Crucifixion where He always wears the waist-cloth. Also in the scenes of the punishments in Hell, the bodies of men and women being punished are shown naked in the fire. The bodies of certain saints or martyrs appear entirely naked or with a waist-cloth in the scenes of their martyrdom.[66] Common is the scene of Abba Zossima giving Communion to Mary of Egypt, who is half naked.

The power of Orthodox iconography appears precisely in these instances of the naked. The iconographer, having subjugated matter to the spirit, created bodies of such form that truly no earthly or carnal thing was implied but only lead one to the high idea, which they seek to express through them. When one sees, for example, the naked Christ in the Jordan of the mosaic of the Baptism in Daphni and in Hosios Loukas near Levadeia, or of the wall-painting in the Perivleptos church of Mystra (plate 9), he

[61] Bettini, *Mosaici antichi,* illustr. CIII.

[62] Oto Bihalji-Merin, *Fresques et Icones,* illustr. 39, 44.

[63] Millet, *Mistra,* illustr. 37.

[64] C. Kalokyris, *The Byzantine Wall-paintings,* illustr. X, 1.

[65] Cf. e.g. the Laurentian codex VI, 23. See also *Early Christian and Byzantine Art,* Baltimore, No. 725 and illustr. CIV.

[66] The naked are also found in the scenes from the Old Testament, e.g. the creation and fall of Adam and Eve, the intoxication of Noah, and others. See Bettini, *op. cit.,* illustr. LIV, LV, LIX. Naked or half-naked are also the children in the Palm Sunday scene, and Christ as an infant in the scene of his bath (Birth of Christ).

is not overcome by the idea of nakedness, but is rather overcome by the idea which the representation expresses. The sense of nakedness, as such, in its natural context, of course, has been neutralized by the spiritual power of Orthodox art. Through this power of the spirit, the figures appear dematerialized, the bodies ἄσαρκα (without flesh), clothed τὴν δόξαν τῶν ἐπουρανίων (in the glory of the heavenly things). To achieve this, the style of Orthodox iconography resorts to certain daring anti-realistic designs. The sides of the thorax are stylized with strong arches, the chest with uniform corresponding curves, the knees are in the shape of an eight, etc. Such as we see in the body of Christ in the scenes of the Baptism (plate 9), of the Crucifixion, and others. Thus, here again the order of stylization follows the general principle of avoiding the strict anatomical reality in order to serve the ideal of disembodiment (Entkörperlichung), which permits the exaltation of the spiritual nucleus, the expression of which is the primary purpose of this art.

In our iconography there are also instances in which certain bodies are painted with an over-emphasis of certain members or parts. This we meet mainly in the representations of hell where some members, related to committed sins, are drawn much larger than necessary, for the purpose of indicating directly and more impressively their characteristics. Thus, in the mosaic of the Punishments in the Basilica of Torcello (12th century),[67] certain bodies in the fire have their stomachs swollen and falling low, to indicate the sin of gluttony for which they are being punished.[68] The same is true with other parts of the bodies connected with sins in the scene of the Punishments in the church of the Apostles (15th century) in Kandanos, Crete, in the church of Panayia (middle aisle) in Kritsa, in the Refrectory of the Monastery of Laura on Mount Athos, and others.[69]

The anti-realistic iconography of sacred persons is completed by the whole appearance of their garments. Even these, of course, are fashioned in agreement with the general principle of Orthodox iconography, by which the major premise of spirituality is served. The garments project or signify the spiritual bodies of

---

[67] It is a section of the scene of the Second Coming.
[68] See colored picture in Grabar, *Peinture byzantine*, p. 120.
[69] Millet, *Athos*, illustr. 149. Cf. also *Mistra*, illustr. 80, 1 etc.

the saints covered by them. And because such bodies, naturally, are not visible, the garments with their entire form become an expression of them. Because of this, simple folds and their wider overlaps do not have the so-called naturalness, that is, they are not like those shapes which garments receive when covering the human body. Not only this, but in certain rarer instances, the folds of the clothing do not correspond completely with the covered members of the bodies. In these instances, tunics, mantles, cloaks, etc. are lapped and folded, if not unrelated to the mass and the movements of the members of the bodies under them, at least more and more intensely than is naturally imposed by their mass or their movement.[70] We note this here because very often even this is misunderstood and is regarded as a weakness of the painters. Of course, the natural in the design of the folds of the garments is precisely the indication of the mass of the bodies and of the movements of their members. Quite often, however, the over-emphasis of the order of stylization which the folds receive to convey transcendence and the whole disposition for exalting in every way the supernatural truth, legitimatize and justify their anti-naturalistic formation.

In the older works especially (or even in the later works following older originals) the foldings of the garments are emphatically lineal. Vertical lines of a darker color than the garments, often going parallel, indicate the folds (plate 2). By this means the clothes attain a certain flatness and seem to be deprived of plasticity, which they especially receive later. Characteristic samples of this type of foldings are the mosaics of St. Demetrius in Salonika (7th cent.) and especially the one showing the saint between the Bishop John and the Eparch Leontius.[71] We have similar lineal foldings in the mosaics of Justinian and Theodora with their court in St. Vitalius of Ravenna (6th century),[72] in the procession of martyrs moving toward Christ in the new church of St.

---

[70] See e.g. the mantle of Christ in the Resurrection of the church of the Theotokos in the village of Lampiotes, Crete, in 'Εκκλησία, Easter, 1960. See also C. Kalokyris, *The Byzantine Wall-paintings*, illustr. XIX (angel).

[71] See G. and M. Sotiriou, Ἡ Βασιλικὴ τοῦ ʽΑγίου Δημητρίου Θεσσαλονίκης (The Basilica of St. Demetrius of Salonika). Cf. also Volbach-Hirmer, *op. cit.*, illustr. 217, and Grabar, *Peinture byzantine*, p. 50.

[72] Volbach-Hirmer, *ibid.*, illustr. 164-167 (in color).

Apollinarius of the same city (6th century),[73] and in the scenes of the life of Christ in the same church.[74] In the following periods, however, the folds in the clothing become well-curved and in relief (rendered particularly with a great deal of freedom), and plasticity becomes a characteristic of the garments. Such a marvelous draping of the garments is especially that of the mosaics in Daphni (11th century). By contrast to the lineal folding of certain garments observed here, however, the prophets in the dome, the Apostles in the Koimesis, the angels (especially in the scene of Joakeim and Anna praying and of the Birth of Christ), St. John before the Cross and the many other sacred persons wear garments of such fine form that they remind one, without doubt, of the draping garments on the statues of classical antiquity[75] (plate 4). From this viewpoint another successful draping of garments is in the mosaics in the Monastery of Chora (Kahrie Djami) in Constantinople (14th century)[76] and in the wall-paintings of the south chapel of the same monument,[77] which contributes especially to the slenderness, to the elegance and to the whole spiritual nobility of the figures.[78] Of undoubtedly exceptional interest for its smoothness and fine curvature is the folding in the garments of the sacred figures in the chapel of St. Euthemius[79] beside the church of St. Demetrius of Salonika, in the church of St. Catherine in the same city, and in the scenes of the Protaton

---

[73] *Ibid.*, illustr 55. Cf. also the older Corrado Ricci, *Ravenna*, Bergamo, illustr. 59, for the entire procession.

[74] *Ibid..* illustr. 61-86. Cf. the lineal folds of the mosaics in the Nea Moné of Chios such as e.g. of the Crucifixion (the women), of Lazarus, etc. See Orlandos, *Monuments byzantins de Chios*, Athens, 1930, illustr. 19, 23.

[75] Millet, *Daphni*, at the end of the book.

[76] Th. Schmitt, "Kahrie-Dzami," in the Bulletin (Isvestija) of the imperial Russian archaeological institute of Constantinople, vol. XI, Sofia, 1906. Color pictures in Grabar, *Peinture byzantine*, pp. 113, 137.

[77] For the wall-paintings of the chapel (with their identification) see P. Underwood in Dumbarton Oaks Papers 9, 10 of 1956, 11 of 1957 f. See especially the foldings in the famous Descent into Hades in 9, 10, of 1956, illustr. 66.

[78] The same is true for the mosaics of the Holy Apostles church in Salonika, with the only difference being that here as in the Monastery of Chora (Kahrie-Djami), we do not observe the delicateness of the folds as we have in the above mentioned mosaics of Daphni.

[79] G. and M. Sotiriou, *Album, op. cit.,* illustr. 93B, 83.

church on Mount Athos[80]. No less significant are the Byzantine monuments of Serbia during the 13th and 14th centuries, which of course are undoubtedly under the influence of Constantinople and Salonika. Thus we note the fine curves of the many-fold garments of the saints in the wall-paintings of Sopotchani (1260-1265) [81] and especially of the holy Apostles in the scene of the Koimesis of the Theotokos[82] (plate 8), as well as the amazing freedom and grace expressed in the clothing of the Apostles of the same scene and of the raising of Lazarus of Gratchanitsa (1321),[83] whose fringes are especially emphasized by the orderly waving in geometrical figures of the foldings[84] (plate 8).

A characteristic of these folds in the clothing of Orthodox iconography is precisely the principle of shaping them geometrically in order and usually in agreement to the mass of the bodily members under them. This principle, despite all the free formation of the clothing, deprives the folds of naturalness (that is, the slavish imitation of the form of the garment of everyday man) and offers a particular spirituality and grace both to the clothing and to the body it covers. The anti-realistic lighting contributes especially to this supra-sensual impression of the clothing. This lighting is usually achieved by a light (whitish, rosy,

---

[80] Millet, *Athos*, illustr. 12, 4; 13, 3; 30, 2; etc. Cf. also Xyngopoulos, Μανουὴλ Πανσέληνος (Manuel Panselenos), Athens, 1956, (illustr. 1, 2, 13). Also C. Kalokyris, *Athos, Themes of Archaeology and Art*, chp. 2.

[81] The iconographer of this work must certainly have come from Constantinople as indicated by his whole style. Moreover, from the preserved signatures the names are known of Greek artists who came from Salonika and Constantinople to paint the walls of churches in Serbia and to teach the Serbs during the reign of King Miloutin. The wall-paintings of Sopotchani are a Byzantine work; the opinion of O. Mihaldji-Merin (repeating the views of the earlier Serbs) that these belong to the "peinture monumentale medievale serbe" (according to the French translation of the book by A. Daussy) is of course incorrect (Fresques et Icones — notes explicatives — between no. 38 and 39, see also p. 12).

[82] *Ibid.*, illustr. 39. See also the similar scene (the empty tomb of the Theotokos) in Stoudenitsa (1314), illustr. 30.

[83] The iconographer of this work is associated with Salonika and particularly with the Protaton church of Mount Athos.

[84] Petcović, *Le peinture Serbe du moyen âge*, vol. I, Beograd, 1930, illustr. 50, and color picture in Grabar, *La peinture byzantine*, p. 149. The scene of Lazarus see in O. Mihaldji-Merin, *op. cit.*, illustr. 57.

etc.) color, that is, by the color of the garment, but in a lighter tone or even by a complementary color placed in diagonal shapes or in spots at the prominent points or at the edges of the folds and along their course. The strong lighting especially on the darker garments not only contributes to the impression of the dematerialization of the forms, but also emphasizes the radiance and the splendour of the spiritual world, which it symbolizes and co-extends to the creation of the whole transcendent atmosphere of iconography.[85] By means of successful coloring and this wisely calculated lighting in the necessary and particular points (in which truly the Byzantines have proven to be unique), the clothing is made truly ethereal. This we see, for example, in the often mentioned angels of the Liturgy in the Perivleptos church in Mystra, in the Apostles of the above mentioned Koimesis of the Theotokos in Gratchanitsa and of the Holy Communion in the Monastery of Vrontessi in Crete, and in a great number of other monuments.[86] Other times again in the mosaics and particularly in the portable icons (primarily of Christ and the Theotokos) the lighting of the garment is gold, achieved in the prominent parts by the use of oval, rectangular or usually triangular golden shapes from the sides of which gold lines move to indicate the folds (see the mantle of Christ in the famous icon of Michael Damascenos, "Touch me not") (plate 38). From among the mosaic garments, lighted in the same manner, the mantle of Christ of the Descent into Hades in the Nea Moné of Chios (11th cent.)[87] with the comb-like lighting,[88] the maphorium of the Theotokos in the scene of the Birth of Christ in the Capella Palatina in Palermo (12th century),[89] are only some examples at random.[90] Finally,

---

[85] See e.g. the lighting of the garments of the angels in the Birth of Christ of Daphni.

[86] C. Kalokyris, *The Byzantine Wall-paintings of Crete*, p. 98.

[87] Orlandos, *Monuments byzantine de Chios*, illustr. 19, 20, 3.

[88] This lighting is applied chiefly from this period on.

[89] Demus, *The Mosaics of Norman Sicily*, London, 1949.

[90] From the large number of panel icons we note as evidence two of the Virgin Mary and Child (particularly for the mantle of Christ) in the Benaki Museum (Xyngopoulos, *Catalogue*, illustr. 36, no. 47, 48) and the mantle of Christ in the famous icon showing the Theotokos holding Child and called "The Perivleptos" (14th century), found in the church of St. Clement of Ochrid (O. Mihaldji-Merin, *op. cit.*, illustr. 69, in color).

in some instances, the anti-realistic lighting, which is made geometrically more intense, reaches the point of being indicated by the particularly impressive large rounded spots placed on the clothing just at the points where there is a corresponding rounded or curved member of the body. Such form of clothing we have in the mosaics of San Marco of Venice. In the dome of the church depicting the Ascension, most of the figures (angels, prophets, apostles, personifications) have such rounded lighting upon their mantles at the thighs, elbows, knees, and breast.[91] In the scene of the unbelief of Thomas, the mantle of the doubting Apostle, folded with direct lines and lighted in the same manner at the slackened left leg, is lighted at the projecting right leg by three successive clear geometric shapes, that is, the large circle corresponding to the hip-joint (the buttock), the trapezium corresponding to the thigh, and the circular section corresponding to the lower leg.

The garments of the sacred persons are worthy of examination from the viewpoint of color also. Even though one observes a colorful variety and wealth, the clothing does not have colors or repulsive liveliness, but on the contrary, their use is characterized by undertone and good taste. Delicate shades of the red, blue, and green are consecrated for the garments of Christ and the Theotokos, while for the other sacred persons the shades are always less pronounced. A multitude of such examples of bright and luminous colored garments (of tones always agreeable to the climate of high nobility in iconography) we have in the Byzantine and post-Byzantine portable icons.[92] The modesty of the colors is characteristic in the mosaics. Besides the gold which is chiefly used for the garment of Christ and for the imperial purple robes, there are the usual shades of the white (gray), the green, the red, and the blue. The garments of the saints, in the above mentioned procession in St. Apollinarius Nuovo of Ravenna, are white. In the garments of the Apostles in the dome (the Ascen-

---

[91] Bettini, *Mosaici antichi*, illustr. XVI, XXI. See also illustr. LXVIII, LXX, etc.

[92] There is an infinite bibliography and an infinite number of examples regarding these. By way of indication, see G. and M. Sotiriou, Εἰκόνες τῆς Μονῆς Σινᾶ (Icons of the Monastery of Sinai), Athens, 1956, 1958, and Walter Felicetti-Liebenfels, *Geschichte der byzantinischen Ikonenmalerei*, Olten-Lausanne, 1956.

sion) of St. Sophia of Salonika (plate 33), of the prophets in the dome of Daphni, etc., besides the use of different colors, one general light-gray tone predominates. This is owed to the prevailing large whitish or gray luminous spots, lines, etc., by which the shades of the many-fold garments are emphasized. Thus, in the general unity of the light the impression of the principal colors of the garments is diminished. This, however, in no way constitutes a shortcoming, that is, this does not create the impression of a cold monotony of a single color. On the contrary, this art succeeded by the unity of imposed color — vibrated by the calculated shades of the foldings — in connecting even more the sacred figures to each other, ordering them in the higher unity of a composition in form, by which their spiritual purity is indisputably characterized and emphasized. This spiritual purity and the relatedness of the saints in that same purity, which is marked in our iconography by the pouring of light upon their forms, is also expressed by the use of white garments. How correct this is can be seen in the Gospel codex of Rossano (Calabria) of the 6th century wherein, among others, the parable of the ten Virgins is depicted. Here, while the five foolish virgins are shown wearing many-colored, bright and impressive garments, the five prudent virgins, on the contrary, are shown clothed in modest white garments, symbols of their purity and their whole virtue.[93]

Whatever we said above for the clothing in the mosaics of St. Sophia of Salonika and in Daphni is also applicable, more or less, to the clothing in other monuments, such as the mosaics of Hosios Loukas near Levadeia, of St. Sophia in Constantinople, of Capella Palatina in Palermo, of the Holy Apostles in Salonika, and of the Monastery of Chora (Kahrie) in Constantinople. Certainly there are differences among the clothing of these chronologically distant and stylistically separated monuments, but common to them all, more or less, are the soft and modest colors, the lack of "loud," acute tones of red, of blue, etc. This is so because even in the cases where, for example, the red or blue colors are used, these are placed in softer tones (reddish, rosy, or bluish), or they are mitigated by the lively whitish lights, or they are restrained by the juxtaposition of a color harmonious to these in the pro-

---

[93] A Muñoz, *Codex purpureus Rossanensis,* Roma, MCMVII, illustr. IV. Color picture in Grabar, *Peinture byzantine,* p. 163.

jected garment of the same or of another person. Always the position of these colors is considered in the whole composition and especially in relation to the background of iconography. Thus, for example, in the bright blue maphorium of the infant-holding Theotokos, pictured between John II Comnenus and Irene in the mosaic in the narthex of St. Sophia in Constantinople (12th century), the impression of the bright color is mitigated not only because it is connected to the blue which is on the garments of the imperial couple, but also because the mantle and the nimbus of Christ, whom the Theotokos holds before her, is of a gold color, as the whole background of the scene is also gold. In other words, the blue maphorium of the Virgin, emphasized in the gold atmosphere of the mosaic and restrained by the all-gold garments of Christ, is fully harmonized in the entire composition. This succession of a gold background, blue garment and gold infant we have also in the mosaic (to mention another example from Constantinople) of the enthroned Christ between Constantine Monomachus and Zoe (11th century), with the difference, of course, that the position of the gold Child-Christ is here taken by the great golden Gospel which the Lord holds.[94] In the same century, in the Nea Moné of Chios, the deep-blue mantle of Christ in the scene of the Descent into Hades is connected and harmonized to the gold background of the scene by means of the gold lineal folds, as we have seen, and by the gold comb-like lights upon it.[95] The following century, in the mosaic of the Birth of Christ in the Capella Palatina of Palermo, the blue maphorium of the Virgin became all-gold from the gold lighting poured upon it. Thus, it was connected most harmoniously to the gold mountain and cave and to the whole gold background of the scene. As in Daphni so also here the impression of the color of the garment (blue) is underplayed, while the color of the lighting (gold) dominates as it is poured everywhere to unify the entire composition.[96]

We have similar observations also for the colors of the garments in the wall-paintings. However, despite their advantages

---

[94] Th. Whittemore, *The Mosaics of St. Sophia at Istanbul, The Mosaics of the Narthex*, Oxford, 1933, p. 7. Color picture in Grabar, *Peinture byzantine*, p. 99.

[95] Color picture in Grabar, *Peinture byzantine*, p. 108.

[96] Color picture in *op. cit.*, p. 130.

over the mosaics on account of the direct use of the colors and the facility of the detail brush, the garments in the best and most classical works of this kind are rendered with soft colors corresponding fully, even here, to the nobility of the represented persons, and thus contributing to the whole transcendent atmosphere of iconography. Here also, however, the necessary bright colors of the garments — corresponding to the realistic spirit of the period — are excellently harmonized in the composition with the blue background, which dominates in the wall-paintings instead of the gold.[97] In the wall-paintings of Sopotchani,[98] (to be sufficed only with this), coinciding chronologically with the summit of the Palaiologian renaissance (second half of the 13th century), the garments of exceptional technical execution came to complete the picture of spirituality, which the physiognomies as a whole manifested. The Apostles here, for example, who approach in order to receive Communion from the hands of Christ, all wear blue tunics with strong lighting at the fringes, while their softly draping mantles are interchanged harmoniously in coloring of iodine, green and bluish, and thus receive a wondrous brilliance with the abundant lighting from their own colors but in opened tones. Through the blue tunics, the Apostles are connected to the blue-green ground upon which they walk, while through their iodine-lighted mantles they are connected to the yellow background before which (in remembrance of the gold of the art of mosaics) their bodies are projected. Thus, the Apostles, shining in their mantles and having ὑψηλαῖς ταῖς φρεσὶ (their minds exalted) — as indicated by the formation of their faces full of exaltation, approach to enjoy ξενίας Δεσποτικῆς καὶ ἀθανάτου Τραπέζης, (the hospitality of a Royal and immortal Table). It is certainly not necessary to repeat here what significance for Orthodox worship is held by this challenge to the faithful to experience the emotion of the Mystery of Holy Eucharist as it is achieved by the shapes and colors of art.

---

[97] The wall-paintings of Santa Maria Antiqua of Rome, of Castelseprio of Milano, of St. Sophia of Ochrid, of St. Panteleimon in Nerezi, of Sopotchani (Serbia), of the chapel of St. Euthemius beside the church of St. Demetrius of Salonika, of the chapel in the Monastery of Chora in Constantinople, of the Protaton, of Stoudenitsa, of the churches of Kastoria, of Mystra, of Crete, of Rhodes, of Mt. Athos (as the Lavra) and certainly a multitude of other monuments offer such exceptional examples.

[98] Color picture in *Fresques et Icones, op. cit.,* illustr. 44.

2. *The Environment in Iconography*

That which characterizes the faces, the naked parts and the garments in our iconography characterizes also the whole environment, as it will become clear. The elements of form in the environment are primarily limited to the manner by which the space is represented in the iconographies and in the background wherein the figures, the iconographic themes or their incidents are ordered.

At first we observe generally that Orthodox iconography never attempted to represent the environment in which the sacred physiognomies and the sacred scenes appear according to the naturalistic manner. Never was the surrounding space given the same value and significance as a basic expressive means of art as was given especially by Western art since the Renaissance, or rather since the period of Giotto. The attitude of the bodies, their movements, their gestures, together with the value which they possess of themselves, as well as a few other general elements in the representation, were sufficient to indicate the space of the active persons in the sublime Orthodox art, without the necessity of amassing helpful technical means[99] formed especially for this purpose. The principal interest in our iconography, therefore, is limited to the sacred persons, while the architectural patterns, the mountains, etc. in the background of the icons are always subordinated to these persons who hold the dominant position. Thus, the background does not possess self-sufficiency, that, is, it does not present a formation independent of the persons, but is always integrated with them. In the Baptism, for example, Christ is in the middle of the river Jordan, while the mountains in the background are arranged orderly from the left and the right of Christ, that is, they are harmonized according to Him. In the Burial Lament, the body of Jesus with the Theotokos and the other persons holds again the center of the composition, while behind on the left and the right, the rocks of the landscape are designed, and in the empty space behind Christ the Cross is raised. Thus, the environment is rendered on the basis of the central person of the icon. In the Descent into Hades likewise, the background is filled by two precipitously graded rocks, while in the empty space between these the figure of Christ dominates.[100] The same is true also for

---

[99] Such a means, e.g. is the perspective, which constitutes a technical means and not an artistic means.

[100] See example in Xyngopoulos, *Catalogue, op. cit., illustr.* 18, 50, 51, etc.

the scene of the Mocking, the Touch of Thomas, etc. , where behind Christ large architectural patterns are always formed to exalt His figure, while smaller architectural patterns are formed at the sides.[101]

All of the above elements, which of course are not taken actually (as in the secular and especially in the Renaissance art) but only by accommodation, usually determine that which we call *space* in Orthodox iconography. As it has been made clear already, in order to render this space, the active persons are drawn on the first plane of the icon, while of the above mentioned elements only the necessary ones are summarily used for the historical setting of the scene, such as buildings, trees, rocks, mountains, etc. Their purely symbolical and not realistic meaning is also indicated by their whole design. A little green, a few roses (not usually) and four rivers denote the Garden of Eden. A ciborium surrounded by a railing symbolizes the church. The mountainous landscapes are always indicated by precipitous rocks stylized with escalations, whose stylization is intensified at the peaks (plate 23). A wall with embattlements and gateways, e.g., drawn behind the scene of the Crucifixion, indicates the city of Jerusalem. An event which has taken place within a closed space is usually pictured without it; the space is not of interest, but the event itself is. Thus, e.g., the visit of the Theotokos to Elizabeth is represented *outside*[102] some house, before which both women stand. The Last Supper also is represented before architectural patterns often connected by the red Byzantine cloth which covers the open space between them.[103] The Annunciation of the Theotokos, [104] the Caress

---

[101] Cf. also the scene of the Koimesis of the Theotokos where to the left and right of the Virgin and on a second plane, structures are painted, while between them, in the empty space, Christ is represented bearing the soul of His mother.

[102] Despite the written declaration of the Evangelist Luke (1:49) that the Theotokos εἰσῆλθεν εἰς τὸν οἶκον Ζαχαρίου καὶ ἠσπάσατο τὴν Ἐλισάβετ (entered into the house of Zacharius and saluted Elizabeth).

[103] See e.g. in the codices such as Tetraevangelium of the National Library of Paris, Paris Gr. 54, in Millet, *Recherches, op. cit.*, fig. 277.

[104] It is understood that we are not talking here of the later period where especially in post-Byzantine panel icons, elements from the West were introduced among which there was also the representation of a related scene within the house-space.

of her parents, and other internal scenes, are painted in the same manner.

A result of these symbolic and accommodating elements of the environment is that there are no regular analogies of the objects of space nor the correct and logical relationship of the persons toward them. Behind the persons, for example, in certain instances slopes of a mountain are represented; the walking figures may have one foot on one of these slopes and the other foot upon another slope. The horses, for example, bearing the Magi to the Birth of Christ, may have the two legs upon one slope in the background and the other two drawn upon another slope situated directly behind the cave. In the Birth of Christ at Daphni, the praising angels (the two on each side of the rays of the star) stand behind the peak of the rocky landscape. This does not obstruct their arms from extending above the summit-line and thus giving the impression that they are above the cave.[105]

In the older Christian art but even in certain instances in the Byzantine, the anti-realistic characteristics are stronger. The successive incidents, for example, of one and the same theme are not separated between them but are presented without separation and upon the same plane, leaving it up to the spectator to separate them in his mind and to find their chronological coherence. This we have also in the works of sculpture art (as in the sarcophagi)[106] and in the miniatures of Byzantine manuscripts.[107] Later, however, the various incidents of a represented scene are usually separated by the folds of the ground in each of which one or more incidents are placed, as we see, for example, in the representation of the Birth of Christ (Christ-Theotokos, Angels, Magi, Shepherds, Scene of the Bath, etc.), of the Transfiguration, of Lazarus, etc. By these folds the meaning of the background is also offered here. But in many instances these folds do not exist; the rendition of the background then is made by the *superposition* of the represented figures, that is, by the

---

[105] C. Kalokyris, *The Birth of Christ, op. cit.,* illustr. 1.

[106] See examples in Volbach-Hirmer, *op. cit.,* illustr. 37, 40, and others.

[107] As in the Greek manuscript 699 of the Library of the Vatican containing the Christian cosmography of Cosmas the Indicopleustes, where the conversion of the Apostle Paul on his way to Damascus is found and in which he is also represented in four unseparated incidents. See in relation to this Grabar, *Peinture byzantine,* pp. 165-167.

placing of a row of persons precisely above the similar row at the lower part of the composition to denote that it is found on a second plane. Thus, for example, angels in the Second Coming are projected above the Apostles; Patriarchs in Paradise are drawn above Peter and the Thief; soldiers in the Child-slaying are represented some above the others, etc. But these figures situated above — that is, those represented on a higher level or those usually on a second and third plane clearly distinguished by the folds of the landscape—are not stylized always on a smaller scale, as it is demanded by the representation of the distances according to the logical laws of perspective; rather they are represented on the same scale as the lower or often even on a larger scale. For example, in the representations of the Birth of Christ, above the scene of the new-born child's bath and on a second plane next to the Child, the Virgin is represented on a larger scale, whereas, according to the logical laws of perspective, she should have been drawn smaller, as being situated further away.[108] That is to say that in iconography the so-called principle of ἀνεστραμμένης προοπτικῆς (reversed perspective) is applied, according to which the persons and things lying further away are drawn larger while the nearer are drawn smaller.[109] This constitutes a result of the whole spirit of Orthodox painting seeking to avoid the natural reality and being concerned for the spiritual truth. Also, in agreement with this spirit is the practice in our art of placing in the composition the events and their incidents in the order of their value as primary and secondary, that is, in order of their historical and religious significance. In such case, a person or an event μείζονος σημασίας (of greater significance) is represented on a larger scale than the other persons or events, regardless of the position (that is, the plane) on which it is found in the composition. Thus, Orthodox iconography indicates in some manner by the size of its dimensions those persons about whom worship is centered. The Theotokos in the Birth, as we have seen (pl. 4), the angel who sits on the rock in the related representation, Christ on the Cross, Christ in the Descent into Hades, Christ among the Myrrh-bearers, etc., is often of much larger proportions than the

---

108 C. Kalokyris, *The Birth of Christ*, illustr. II, IX, X, XII.

109 See offhand P. Mouratoff, *Les icones Russes,* Paris, 1927, p. 107, and O. Wulff, *Altchristliche und Buzantinische Kunst,* I, Berlin, 1914, p. 168, and Millet, in Michel's *Histoire de l'art,* pp. 289 f.

nearby persons. As examples we cite the Christ in the scene of the Descent into Hades in the church of St. John (position Φώτης) in Yerakari, Crete, whose proportions are three times larger than those of the raised dead at His sides.[110] Also the Crucified Christ of San Marco in Venice[111] is larger than the soldier, piercing Him and the one giving Him vinegar, but in comparison to the soldiers casting lots for the mantle under the cross, whose representation is a secondary iconographic incident in the whole scene, Christ's is the largest figure.

But it would be an error if it were thought that the background in our iconography was always determined by the manner noted above. Three-dimensional space is not at all unknown to it. The Hellenistic branch of Christian art offered to it elements of three-dimensional space, as we see in the monumental painting and in the manuscripts. These elements were revived and used widely during the rebirth of iconography after the Iconoclast controversy and especially at the time of the Macedons and the Comneni when, as it is known, a great turn was realized toward the ancient Greek models of art and literature. With the other elements from reality, which Byzantine art then received, it also accepted elements for the representation of space, and thus enriched its related ancient Hellenistic tradition.[112] This rebirth was continued and strengthened during the period of the Palaeologoi which likewise looked vigorously to the classical ideals. The realistic spirit of those years was also reflected in the representation of space and of the third dimension in general in the then contemporary Orthodox iconography, as we shall see below. From this period then the three-dimensional space was a usual thing in the wall-paintings as well as in the post-Byzantine portable icons, of which some are, for many reasons, more withdrawn to the related influence of Western art. But as it becomes clear from at least the best works of monumental painting, Orthodox iconography succeeded in enrolling even the elements of space to its purely spiritual form and in assimilating it under its strong power of form (plate 16).

Characteristic examples of space appearing in this way in

---

[110] C. Kalokyris, *The Byzantine Wall-paintings,* illustr. XXI.

[111] Bettini, *op. cit.,* illustr. XXIV.

[112] As that e.g. of Ravenna. See mosaics: Good Shepherd in the Mausoleum of Galla Placidia; Hospitality of Abraham in St. Vitalius.

iconography we have already from the 10th century as, for example, in the mosaic of the Child-holding and enthroned Theotokos between Constantine the Great and Justinian in the narthex of St. Sophia of Constantinople[113] (foot-stool, throne, position of Emperors), in the mosaics of Daphni (Birth, Baptism, etc.), of Palermo (Capella Palatina: Birth, and others). Then there are many such examples in the wall-paintings of Sopotchani (as in the Koimesis), of Salonika (e.g. in the recently cleaned scenes in the church of St. Catherine), in the mosaics of the Monastery of Chora in Constantinople (as in the Census of Cyrenius) and in the wall-paintings of its chapel (as in the Healing of the Daughter of Jarius) in the already mentioned, on another occasion, Macedonian monuments (as e.g. those on Mount Athos), etc. Besides the monumental painting, the miniatures also of those exceptional manuscripts from the period of the Macedons (which copy the ancient painting) constitute more interesting examples.[114]

C. THE REALISTIC FORM IN ORTHODOX ICONOGRAPHY

Presupposing whatever has been said before, we shall now examine the subject of the realistic form in our iconography, that is, the form and the significance which realism has in Orthodox art.

We have said at first that Orthodox iconography is an art purely idealistic, interested in the spiritual ideals and in the reality beyond this world. This truth is expressed by its artistic creations from the first Christian years. Besides this, however, already from the earlier years, realism appeared in Christian iconography under the influence of Hellenistic art (Hellenistic branch of Christian art). This element became in it a means of expression; it

---

113 Wittemore, *The Mosaics of St. Sophia at Istanbul,* p. 31.

114 See the codex Paris. Gr. 510 of the 9th century containing a collection of the Homilies of Gregory Nazianzus (vision of Hezekiah); especially the famous Greek Psalter 139 of the 10th century in the National Library of Paris (the sick Hezekiah, the crossing of the Red Sea); the Scroll of Joshua in the Vatican Library; 431 also of the 10th century; the Gospel 5 of the Iberians from the 13th century, and others. Cf. H. Omont, *Miniatures des plus anciens manuscrits Grecs de la bibliothèque nationale du VIe au XIVe siècle,* Paris, 1929, illustr. IX, XI, etc. Likewise (III) illustr. XX, XXVIII, XXXVI, LVIII, and K. Weitzmann, *Die byzantinische Buchmalerei des IX und X Jahrhunderts,* Berlin, 1953, and *The Joshua Roll—a Work of the Macedonian Renaissance,* Princeton, 1948.

served to make clear precisely the necessary subordination of the material to the spiritual, the worldly reality to the divine reality — a thing which Christian Faith considers as fundamental. Certainly the great concern of this art is directed to the world above the merely human things, but even so the present world constitutes for it something taken for granted. Also, man who has a mortal body and an immortal soul can partake of both worlds. Thus, just as religion is interested in both the reality of the world and in the reality of God, so also is art. Furthermore, art like religion places in the first degree the heavenly reality, in which τὸ πολίτευμα ἡμῶν ὑπάρχει (our citizenship is), but at the same time is not indifferent to the life in this world, which becomes a presupposition for the attainment of the heavenly life. Christ, moreover, and the saints participated in both worlds. They, of course, belong to the world of eternity, but through their historical existence they are also related to the present world. Thus, the elements of expressing the natural reality, that is, that which we call realism, are justifiably made from the beginning integral parts of iconography.

Orthodox iconographers have these things in mind when they represent the bodies of the saints and also the Lord Himself, who σὰρξ ἐγένετο (became flesh) and as God-Man completed His world-saving work. Moreover, the human form was essential in art because otherwise (as for example in utter symbolism or in intense abstraction) iconography would not have been understood by men. But the work and purpose of iconography was always not to represent the present reality in itself, but rather to be subordinated to the other, the true reality, by which it is ennobled and exalted. Thus, specifically, the body does not interest the painting of the Orthodox Church in its fine σωματικὴ (somatic or bodily) meaning, but rather in its significance as ναὸς τοῦ Ἁγίου Πνεύματος (the temple of the Holy Spirit); that is to say, in that form in which spirituality shines and in such a representation in which it is proved that *truly in this body dwells the Holy Spirit* and is not the simple biological body deprived of Grace. Because of this presupposition, the body in our art preserves its ordinary characteristics of form, but these do not correspond to the so-called pure naturalness, they are not rendered according to the strict naturalistic truth. The greater or lesser strictness in such a rendition depends upon that branch of Christian art which influences each time the iconography, or even upon the period to which it belongs (Macedons, Palaeologi, etc.), as we shall see below. Thus the form which the saints have in the works inspired by the Eastern branch of art, appear to be very little faithful to the natural reality. Here the personal truth and the natural moulding of the body are neglected. The contours are emphasized to offer an intensive expressiveness through the almond-shaped eyes designed large beyond proportion, and the stylized rendition of the other characteristics (ears, beard (pl. 5), etc.). Thus the figures appear naturally changed, deviating from the so-called natural beauty. Similarly, the sacred physiognomies do not appear with lively movements, they do not gesticulate, nor are they represented in the space engaged in a natural manner. Rather, they are simply arrayed in order, standing with the face forward in the undetermined, usually, gold or blue background of the compositions. Often the bodies appear unyielding just as the garments covering them (plate 5).

By contrast to the above, in the works inspired by the Hellenistic branch of Christian art, the persons are rendered more naturally true because, instead of the vigorous contours and the intense stylization, the light-shadows dominate to characterize the plastic corporeality and to render the natural mass. Also the bodies are yielding and the foldings of the garments are organic to the sacred forms, which show here graceful positions, beautiful and harmonious movements (plate 6).

But in Orthodox Byzantine iconography the works of the two mentioned branches are not usually presented clearly separated and distinguished from each other, because, as it is known, these influenced each other in the creation of the one Orthodox painting, which united harmoniously in itself both of these branches. This fusion into a unified form, in which the elements of both opposite branches were balanced, was accomplished by Byzantium through its Capital City — especially from the 7th century when the Arabs conquered the Hellenistic centers in the East. But as it often happens in the works of painting, despite the parallel coexistence, some elements of one of the two branches of art appear excelling or at other times entirely domineering. This means that the iconography of those works, for historical and other reasons, underwent the direct and strong influence of the preponderant branch.[115]

---

[115] For example, the Eastern element — of the art of Syria and later of Cappadocia, etc.

After the Iconoclast controversy, of course, the ascetic ideals dominated in the art through the victorious monks. The iconographic type of the ascetic and the saint being formed at this time, despite the abstract expression and the profound spirituality, was a type which did not ignore the realism, as indicated, at least, by the intense leanness of the body, the thoughtful frown, the disorder of the hair and of the beard, and other such things.[116]

The turn to the Hellenistic sources during the period of the Macedons and the Comneni and of the whole climate of the renaissance under the same name is, of course, equivalent to the more realistic appearance of iconography. Thus, this art loves the beautiful heads, the round and healthy faces, the rosy shades of the flesh, the nobility and the sweetness of the eyes and, in one word, the graceful and the elegant, as we see in the miniatures of the manuscripts and in the monumental painting.[117]

The years of the Palaeologi with the lively rebirth of Hellenism and of antiquity[118] are the years of the characteristic realism of Orthodox iconography. The iconographic types remind us often of forms of reality, to which the believer feels that he has a direct familiarity. Thus, e.g., saints, prophets, and hierarchs refer to revered forms of old men with the strong wrinkles of the faces, the expressive eyes, the aquiline noses, the dense eye-brows, the wide mustaches and the heavy beards (plates 11, 12, 13, 17, 37). Women with the oval faces and the prominent cheekbones, or the round faces and the wide chins render analogous types of reality. Young faces and gentle angels presuppose ennobled young physiognomies (plate 34), which were continually brought to the forefront by the research of the illustrated Hellenistic manuscripts. The portrait-realism is completed by the true movements and the ample gestures and even by the whole vigorous emotion of the physiognomies, which often reaches dramatic pathos. The pulsation of life vibrates also the many-person compositions, whose figures are connected by the successful correspondence of the gazes, of the inclinations of the heads and bodies,

---

[116] Grabar, *La décoration byzantine,* Paris, Bruxelles, 1928, p. 19.

[117] See e.g. the beautiful angel in the Vision of Ezekiel of the Codex Paris. Gr. 510 (9th century), *Omont, op. cit.,* LVIII. Cf. also the mosaics of Daphni in Millet, *Daphni,* illustrations.

[118] Ch. Diehl, *La renaissance de l'art byzantin au XIVe siècle,* in *Byzantion,* vol. II (1925), Paris, 1926, pp. 299 f.

and gesticulations — depicting artistically their sublime thoughts.

The realism is continued during the post-Byzantine years and especially in the portable icons, which are relatively influenced by the Western Renaissance, even though the best of them harmonize this element with the Byzantine spiritual tradition (plates 16, 38).

During all the periods of Orthodox art, as mentioned above, the realistic element did not receive the primary position, which it received in the West. That is, as it has already become understood from this entire study, the realism in our iconography did not constitute a slavish imitation and a photographic rendition of living models and, generally, of the so-called natural reality. By its inclusion in the whole transcendent climate of Byzantine iconography — as verified from the beginning — the element of realism was *idealized* and *ennobled*, being changed into an element of high expression especially characteristic of Orthodox art. The point here is the *transformation* of the natural *real'ty* into a higher conception of form, as it also happens precisely, for example, in the best works of poetry and literature. Certainly, it is not necessary to say how much the philosophic disposition and the other theological sensitivity of the artist constituted the main source for such an artistic creation. In this art the believer has the sense of the material, which, however, has been essentially *transformed,*[119] that is, it ἐνεδύθη τὴν ἀθανασίαν, (has put on immortality)[120] (pl. 10). Looking at such sacred works, the believer feels the represented persons to be more familiar through their similarity to him, but, at the same time, he can understand the element of transcendence which constitutes their essential characteristic. This happens because in Orthodox painting we have a *suprapersonal* realism, which receives its impetus from empirical things taken for granted, but which does so for the purpose of a more convenient understanding of the spirit of iconography by the faithful — through a more intense effect upon their senses. Thus, it does not constitute a specific copy of models such as is done as a rule in the religious art of the West, as we have seen. The Orthodox iconographers, by approximating the sacred forms to us through the realistic element, succeeded by an amazing manner in

---

[119] Καὶ ἡμεῖς ἀλλαγησόμεθα (and we shall be changed), I Cor. 15:52.
[120] I Corinthians 15:54.

not depriving these forms of their true spiritual nature, that is, of that element which truly is not ἐκ τοῦ κόσμου τούτου (of this world) (pl. 1). It may be said here, as already observed pertinently for worship,[121] that in these works there is marvelous unity and harmony of "heaven and earth, eternity and time, grace and nature, spirit and flesh, symbol and reality." We may note as expressive examples the Macedonian wall-paintings (such as those of the Protaton, of the chapel of St. Efthemius at St. Demetrius' of Salonika, of Nerezi, of Gratchanitsa, and of Sopotchani), those of Constantinople (we mean those in the Monastery of Chora), those of Mystra (Metropolis, Perivleptos, Pantanassa) and those of many other churches.

In these monuments, while the realism of the faces often expresses an intense drama, the other elements of form are combined with it and fused in such an amazing manner that the spiritual reality remains the superior formative power to unite the opposite elements, to dominate and to bind all the elements of form. In the Burial Lament of Nerezi in Serbia (12th century), for example, the faces are full of life and dramatic truth, but the mould of the bodies, the order of the composition (see e.g. the hand of the Theotokos which comes rhythmically by its curve as a continuation of the circle of the nimbus of Christ), and of the foldings indicate the whole anti-realistic character of the art. In the garments again of the other Palaeologian monuments mentioned above, while one can verify the naturalness in the organic and flexible foldings, this is actually subordinated by the geometric order of the folds, to the transcendent style of Orthodox iconography. In the often mentioned Koimesis of the Theotokos in Sopotchani, we have again natural truth in the faces and in the foldings of the garments as well as in the third dimension of the space. However, the order which unites the figures to one another and orders them according to harmonious groups, the other-worldly expression of the gazes, and the high nobility of the movements and gestures denote the idealization of the composition and its exaltation above earthly things. Christ as twelve years old in the wall-painting in the church of Bojana near Sofia

---

[121] Evangelos D. Theodorou, *The Instructive Value of the Triodeon in Use*, Athens, 1958, pp. 149-150. Cf. by the same author, Τὸ Ὀρθόδοξον Λειτουργικὸν καὶ Μυσταγωγικὸν Κήρυγμα (The Orthodox Liturgical and Mystagogical Sermon), Athens, 1960, p. 45.

(1259) has much natural beauty in the face, but by the entire plastic execution (see left eye) it received a dematerialized and other-worldly character.[122]

By all these things mentioned above, we think, it becomes clear that our ecclesiastical painting attempted to express through the idealized realism the faith of the Church: that the saints, while they lived in the natural world, were through their whole virtuous struggle against evil made worthy of Divine Grace, which exalted and spiritualized their life on earth. Thus, the sacred icons must make perceptible through art this presence of the Grace of the Holy Spirit in the holy physiognomies; it is this Grace which ἐθέωσε (deified)[123] their material element and which, moreover, is inherent in the icons and acts through them. St. John Damascene, in his first oration on the icons, made a most characteristic induction: Οἱ γὰρ ἅγιοι καὶ ζῶντες πεπληρωμένοι ἦσαν πνεύματος ἁγίου καὶ τελευτησάντων αὐτῶν ἡ χάρις τοῦ ἁγίου πνεύματος ἀνεκφοιτήτως ἔνεστι καὶ ταῖς ψυχαῖς καὶ τοῖς σώμασιν ἐν τοῖς τάφοις, καὶ τοῖς χαρακτῆρσι καὶ ταῖς ἁγίαις εἰκόσιν αὐτῶν, οὐ κατ' οὐσίαν, ἀλλὰ χάριτι καὶ ἐνεργείᾳ, (For the saints were filled with the Holy Spirit even when living, and when they died the grace of the Holy Spirit is permanently descended upon their souls and upon their bodies in the graves, and in their characters *and in their holy icons,* not in essence, but in grace and energy.)[124]

---

[122] The painting of Bojana is attributed with certainty to an artist from Constantinople. See Grabar, *La décoration byzantine,* p. 37.

[123] See *The Greek Orthodox Theological Review,* Vol. XII, No. 2 (Winter 1966-1967), pp. 184-185, where this is discussed more generally. (Here we are limited to the case of the realistic form of saints). Christ θεώσας τὸ πρόσλημμα (deifying that which He received) (human nature) (See Vol. XII, No. 2, of this periodical, pp. 203-204) through His Incarnation, offered in His redemptive work the possibility for man to be united with God. (Cf. also Dionysius Areopagite, περὶ οὐρανίου ἱεραρχίας (about the heavenly hierarchy), Migne P.G. 3, 376; θέωσις ἐστιν ἡ πρὸς Θεόν, ὡς ἐφικτόν, ἀφομοίωσίς τε καὶ ἕνωσις (theosis is the assimilation and union with God, as much as possible).

[124] Migne, P.G. 94, 1249 f.

CHAPTER THREE

ICONOGRAPHY AND ORTHODOX WORSHIP

«'Ιησοῦς Χριστὸς χθὲς καὶ σήμερον
ὁ αὐτὸς καὶ εἰς τοὺς αἰῶνας».
('Εβρ. ιγ' 8)

"Jesus Christ the same yesterday,
and today, and forever."
(Hebr. 13:8)

In the previous chapters occasion was given to note the bond of iconography and worship in the Orthodox Church. However, after examination of the content of iconography and of the form in which it appears, it is necessary, more specifically, to include briefly in this chapter its relationship to worship. And this we must do because, as we believe, the understanding of worship is incomplete without the observation and interpretation of the iconography connected with it; also, it is impossible to interpret our sacred art without examining its relationship to worship.

1. Perception and Commentary on Worship

First of all, iconography renders perceptible that which is μυστικῶς (mystically) performed in worship. It is clearly noted that this art seeks to give the form, that is, seeks the μόρφωσιν τῆς σαρκώσεως τοῦ Δεσπότου τῶν ὅλων, τῶν παθημάτων (formation of the Incarnation of the Lord of all, of His sufferings), and of the other events in His life.[1] In other words, iconography attempts with visible, empirical means to contribute to making accessible to the human spirit the mystery of divine Economy, constituting the center of divine worship wherein it is continuously projected and praised. And because the point here is precisely about a mystery, iconography seeks by means of symbols, shapes, and forms largely withdrawn from reality to speak to the soul of the faithful. That is to say, in the manner by which the faithful μυστικῶς τὰ χερουβὶμ εἰκονίζουσιν (represent mystically the Cherubim), so also are the sacred physiognomies represented μυστικῶς (mystically) and not actually.[2]

Only by inference and abstraction upon this anti-realistic and

---

[1] See Chapter Two, A, p. 44 f. Cf. *Triodeon*, ed. Apostolici Diaconia, 142.

[2] That is, as individualities.

in essence mystic art can the believer be helped in understanding the sublime meaning which is expressed through it. Moreover, for a worship which is ἐν πνεύματι καὶ ἀληθείᾳ (in spirit and truth), it was only natural that it seek a more spiritual means of painting to serve its work.

An attempt to make perceivable that which is mystically enacted in worship is also the purpose of the representation of the Divine Liturgy in the niche of the Sanctuary, where Christ is represented ἱερουργῶν ἑαυτὸν (officiating over Himself) as He transmits His Body and His Blood to the Apostles—as we have already noted previously.[3] Because the priest repeats by the liturgical act that which is enacted in Heaven by the Great Hierarch Christ, this ideal performance of the Divine Liturgy in Heaven is represented in the niche as a more perceivable expression of it in the scene in which the Lord receives the Sacred Gifts carried with fear by the angels dressed as deacons—as again we have already noted.[4] To what degree the iconography in the Orthodox Church does not have a decorative purpose, but a liturgical and, generally speaking, a worshipful purpose, appears also from the representation of the liturgical hymn Σιγησάτω πᾶσα σὰρξ βροτεία (All mortal flesh keep silence). Here, as we have noted,[5] art arouses, through the dematerialized forms of the angels, the sacred chill (of emotion) and the actual σιγὴν τῆς σαρκὸς (silence of the flesh)—as worship itself especially demands at that same time (entrance of the Sacred Gifts). When the worshipper sees these other-worldly forms which the skill and the style of this art created (lightning bolts projecting in the shadowy background of the wall-paintings), his whole being is moved by the realization that truly αἱ δυνάμεις τῶν οὐρανῶν σὺν ἡμῖν ἀοράτως λατρεύουσιν (the powers of heaven worship invisibly with us). There is no doubt that if iconography had created forms of worldly beauty it would certainly not have assisted in the perception and understanding of the mystery of worship. Likewise, the application of the worship exhortation to the human body, μηδὲν γήϊνον ἐν ἑαυτῇ λογιζέσθω (think of nothing earthly in itself), would certainly not have been helped by the representation of angels and saints, who would have

---

[3] Chapter One, No. 2, p. 16 f.
No. 2, p. 177 f.
[4] Ibid., p. 17 f.
[5] Ibid., p. 18.

brought to mind not divine but altogether earthly persons. This exhortation alone is capable of signifying the character of Orthodox iconography, its relation to Orthodox worship, but also its entire unrelatedness to the European worldly-minded ecclesiastical painting. Our iconography, being subordinate to the Church and always constituting an expression of Her life of worship, attempts, by arranging even the more realistic elements under a higher spiritual unity of form, to create to the outmost forms which remind one of μηδὲν γήϊνον (nothing earthly).

But this iconography is related to worship not only by making perceivable that which is mystically enacted by it, but also by the more general representation of the scenes of the life of Christ, of the Theotokos, and of the Saints. These representations, and especially those of the struggles of the saints, are not made only ὅπως ἂν καὶ οἱ μὴ εἰδότες γράμματα . . . τῇ θεωρίᾳ τῆς ζωγραφίας μνήμην τε λαμβάνωσι τῆς τῶν γνησίως τῷ ἀληθινῷ δεδουλευκότων ἀνδραγαθίας καὶ πρὸς ἄμιλλαν διεγείρωνται . . . (in order that even those who are not educated would, by the vision of the painting, receive in their memory the courageous exploits of those who genuninely have served the true God and who would be aroused to compete with them), according to Neilos the Ascetic (5th cent.),[6] but also in order that they may be used as the necessary commentaries to the fundamental themes of worship. It is worthy of observation that our iconography does not deviate into details outside the theme, but rather delimits itself to the characteristic events and to their incidents,[7] which are precisely exalted and emphasized by worship. Thus, scenes of the Birth of Christ, of the Passion, and of the Resurrection (about which—as referring to the Divine Economy—worship is primarily concerned), are not missing from any painted church, while it is possible for other scenes such as those of the Lord's miracles or teaching to be missing. Also, the veneration in honor of the Theotokos, which was enriched especially with a hymnody during the period of the Macedonian emperors and the Comneni, dictates iconographic themes, related to this worship. Particularly the exceptional position which worship re-

---

[6] Migne, *P.G.* 79, 577. Regarding the author see in D. Balanos, Πατρολογία (Athens, 1930), 285-287.

[7] It is understood that here we do not mean the details of the iconographic themes especially in the narrative art of the Palaeologi, etc.

serves for the Akathistos Hymn has created the twenty-four iconographic scenes of this hymn, which are developed mainly during the period of the Palaeologi. In relation again to the saints, scenes are drawn depicting their life and usually their martyrdom, which is exalted in the liturgical hymns of worship. The death of the martyr and the representation above it of the hand of Christ offering a crown to the martyr is directly related to the hymns of the liturgy which praise the death of the martyr for Christ. Because the martyr τὰς ἀλγηδόνας καὶ τὰς βασάνους ὑπέστη (suffered the pains and the tortures) for the sake of Christ, he received from Christ in return στέφος τὸ ἄφθαρτον (the incorruptible crown) of his victorious martyrdom. The comprehensive and impressive language of the Orthodox liturgy of worship is here analogous to the imposing language of Orthodox art.

2. Iconography and "Liturgical" (Condensed) Time

It has already been indicated, especially in the recent studies on worship, that time in worship is not considered under the concept of the natural flow of events, that is, of the past, the present, and the future; in worship the past and the future are regarded as a direct present. The point here concerns the so-called "liturgical" or "condensed" (concentré) time about which G. Pidoux[8] wrote a few years ago. That is to say, "most usually in worship, time ceases to exist in the form of past, present, and future, and is changed into a mystical life-experience in which, while eternity is lived in the present, the things of the past and of the future and even the eschatological things, that is, prehistory and the main stations of the redemptive work of Christ, as well as the salutary gifts extending to the last days which flowed from Him, are condensed and lived mystically as alive and present before us."[9] Thus, therefore, in worship "every timely sign of the saving work of the Lord is relived through the lifting of the concept of time."[10]

---

[8] "A propos de la notion Biblique du Temps," in *Revue de Théologie et de Philosophie* (Lausanne, 1952), 120 f. Cf. in this connection the more related study of Savvas Agourides, Χρόνος καὶ Αἰωνιότης ('Εσχατολογία καὶ Μυστικοπάθεια) ἐν τῇ θεολογικῇ διδασκαλίᾳ 'Ιωάννου τοῦ Θεολόγου (Salonika, 1959), 37 f. (Time and Eternity—Eschatology and Mysticism—in the Theological Teaching of John the Theologian). See also Evangelos D. Theodorou, *The Instructive Value of the Triodeon*, 82-86.

[9] E. Theodorou, *The Triodeon*, 83.

[10] Mark Siotes, 'Ιστορία καὶ 'Αποκάλυψις κατὰ τὴν 'Επιστήμην τῆς Καινῆς Διαθήκης (Salonika, 1958) 79 f. (History and Revelation according to the Science of the New Testament).

Also the individual events of religious history are not to be understood as mere occurrences, but as happening mystically and as being active events even today. This means that the one who worships does not merely remember, but lives and actually partakes himself of the life of the Saviour and of His saints.

Byzantine iconography is connected with this meaning of time as it is understood in Orthodox worship. This connection makes the relationship of worship and iconography even greater. Even in iconography time in the mathematical sense is abolished; the sacred persons and events are represented in such a manner that they are συγχρονιζόμενα (contemporized) and appear as belonging to the eternal present, or, to put it otherwise, to eternity—introduced and lived in the present and in every time.

We already know from the history of iconography that a religious event, taking place within a closed space (such as e.g. the Annunciation of the Theotokos, the salutation of Elizabeth by the Theotokos, the Last Supper, etc.), is represented in Byzantine art as if it had taken place outside of this space. Also, we add, in this art those elements (see below) which could determine strictly and in detail the time in which one of these events took place are delimited or even entirely (more rarely) missing. The reason for this is that Orthodox art, being a means of Orthodox worship, is concerned with making it visibly manifest that the spiritual significance of the represented historical event has raised it above any determined space as well as any determined time, that it has escaped the limitations of the space and time of its execution, and that it has acquired infinite extention and duration. That is to say, that one such event which occurred in some particular space and time has received the power, through the active Grace of God, to be continued even today and tomorrow and forever. Orthodox iconography, in other words, looking toward worship, which, as we have said, is not limited to the static remembrance of the sacred persons or events, but rather underlines their living and active presence, rendered its sacred subjects according to an analogous manner. That is, our iconography raised the religious persons and events to one continuous present by releasing them from the unnecessary iconographic elements, which would have characterized and emphasized only their past significance. Thus, the believer is not prevented from feeling that the painted events could take place even today, and that consequently the history of the Passion and the other events in the life of the

Saviour, the achievements of His saints, etc., constitute fundamental subjects not only of the past but also for the present. The Church in worship, narrating through the prayers or singing through her hymns of such events, uses, as is known, present tense expressions, or the adverb σήμερον (today).[11] That is, the Birth of the Lord, His Passion, His Resurrection, etc., are dramatized as events which take place "today."[12] Thus, Christ who is χθὲς καὶ σήμερον ὁ αὐτὸς καὶ εἰς τοὺς αἰῶνας (the same yesterday, today, and forever)[13] — being outside the demands of the categories of space and time—comes even today to us through worship, as He came also to His contemporaries.[14]

Under this particular meaning of the raising of the limits of time in worship we can understand many representations of Byzantine iconography. Sacred persons in mosaics, such as those of Ravenna, of Hagia Sophia in Constantinople,[15] many of Daphni (e.g. in the dome), etc., are depicted against the gold atmosphere of the undetermined background and thus appear released from elements which would limit them in time and space. But through such a manner they may belong to any one period in the past, in the future, and therefore also in the present. In other words, they may be "contemporized" (συγχρονίζονται) each time to make their relation personal to us today and to others tomorrow. For the

---

11 Fr. Heiler, *Urkirche und Ostkirche* (München, 1937), 363. Cf. also Evang. Theodorou, *The Triodeon*, 85 and by the same author, Τὸ Ὀρθόδοξον Λειτουργικὸν Κήρυγμα (The Orthodox Liturgical Sermon), (Athens, 1960), 14.

12 We remind the use of σήμερον in worship as e.g. Σήμερον τίκτει ἡ Παρθένος τὸν ποιητὴν τοῦ παντός . . . (Today the Virgin gives birth to the creator of all . . . (Birth); Σήμερον κρεμᾶται ἐπὶ ξύλου . . . (Today He hangs on a wood . . . (Passion); Σήμερον ὁ Ἅδης στένων βοᾷ . . . (Today Hades bemoaning cries . . . (Descent into Hades); Σήμερον σωτηρία τῷ κόσμῳ γέγονεν· ἄσωμεν τῷ ἀναστάντι ἐκ τάφου . . . (Today salvation was made for the world; let us sing unto the one risen from the grave . . . (Resurrection); etc., etc.

13 Hebrews 13:8.

14 J. Tyciak, *Jahreskranz de Gütte Gottes, Das Jahr der Kirche* (Mainz, 1953), 14. Cf. Evang. Theodorou, *The Instructive Value of the Triodeon*, 84.

15 See examples of the enthroned Christ between Constantine Monomachus and Zoe; the enthroned Theotokos between John II Comnenos and Irene.

eleventh century this is particularly apparent in the mosaics of Nea Moni at Chios, in Hosios Lucas near Levadia, in Daphni, and later in St. Mark's at Venice. The Crucified Christ of Daphni, for example, as he is projected upon the gold atmosphere of the mosaic without particular signs indicating spatial or timely limitations of the scene, becomes timeless—an eternal symbol of the supreme Sacrifice. The characteristic elements of space and time, especially those favored in later periods,[16] which accompanied the event (such as the panorama of the city of Jerusalem behind the Cross, the representation of the two crucified thieves, Golgotha, the soldier giving vinegar and the other lancing the side of Jesus, the incident of the dividing of the garments, etc.) are missing here, or rather are only elementarily indicated for the sake of historical clarity and completeness of the idea which the representation expresses. These elements are a small hill-like rise with the skull of Adam, that is, Golgotha, with the Theotokos and John standing by the Cross. But with Christ, who in worship is crucified today[17] in a mystical manner, the persons of the Theotokos and the beloved disciple who suffer with Him even today may stand together in such an icon. Also below the Cross may be the skull washed by the blood of the Saviour, since it is His blood which cleanses from sin the descendants of Adam who believe in Christ and who receive from Him the gift of immortality. For this reason and from this aspect as well, the representation of the Crucifixion at the Monastery of Daphni, in its simplicity, is incomparable. The κένωσις (kenosis) of the Lord upon the Cross for our salvation is presented by worship as enacted *today* and thus as overcoming the limits of time; iconography represents it here in a similar conquest of time, that is, as an event contemporary to us.

What we said above may be applied to a multitude of other representations as well as to the representation of the child-holding Theotokos depicted alone in the all-gold quarter-sphere of the niche in the Sanctuary of many Byzantine churches. For example, in the famous basilica of Torcello we have one such excellent example of the twelfth century. Standing erect, full-bodied and alone, the Mother of God holding the Christ child is

---

[16] The elements of time exist certainly in the older monuments, but also in the monuments of the Crucifixion contemporary to Daphni, such as in St. Mark's at Venice. See S. Bettini, *op. cit.,* illus. XXIV.

[17] Tyciak, *op. cit.,* 14 f.

raised daringly, as it has been observed,[18] in the middle of the spacious niche, that is, without the usual escort of the archangels on each side of her. As she appears with the divine Child in her arms in the gold air of the mosaic, the Theotokos gives the impression that she is projected into the infinite, that the artist overcame the limitations of time and raised the Incarnation-in-time of the timeless-Logos (for it is this Incarnation that the child-holding Theotokos in the niche expresses) as the unique Event shaping the eternal becoming of history. Out of the infinite heaven, the Theotokos here is, in a sense, performing that well-known royal gesture of presenting the newly-born royal child to the multitudes of citizens standing below. But as the representation appears morphologically beyond time, the joyous proclamation to the people which is understood to follow simultaneously with the presentation of the child, ὅτι ἐτέχθη ἡμῖν σήμερον σωτήρ .. (that today a saviour was born to us), that παιδίον ἐγεννήθη ἡμῖν, Υἱὸς καὶ ἐδόθη ἡμῖν (a Child was born to us, and a Son was given to us), gives one the feeling that it is directed to ourselves who gaze at the icon today, as well as to those who have gazed upon it in the past, and also to those who will gaze upon it in the future. Here, therefore, the "condensed" time of worship is made excellently perceivable by Byzantine art.

The representation of the Last Supper is analogous both elsewhere and in the church of St. Mark's in Venice. As the mosaic representation here depicts upon the gold background only the table of the Supper and the disciples eating with the Lord,[19] it does not confine the beholder λειτουργικῶς (liturgically) only to the determined time of the past when the scene of the Last Supper took place, but rather leads one to the ψυχοτρόφον Τράπεζαν (soul-feeding Table) of the Holy Eucharist, which supports, renews, and deifies,[20] today and tomorrow and every time those who partake of it worthily.

---

[18] Grabar, *La peinture byzantine*, 119 and color plate on p. 121.

[19] Bettini, *op. cit.*, illus. XIV.

[20] Those who communicate worthily θεοῦνται ἠθικῶς τῇ μεθέξει τοῦ θείου (are deified ethically by participation of the divine) as noted by John Karmiris, Σύνοψις τῆς δογματικῆς διδασκαλίας τῆς Ὀρθοδόξου Καθολικῆς Ἐκκλησίας (Synopsis of the Dogmatic Teaching of the Orthodox Church), (Athens, 1957), 57; also by the same author, "Abriss der dogmatischen Lehre der Orthodoxen katholischen Kirche," (from the series: *Die Kirchen der Welt*, B. I.), (Stuttgard, 1959), 68, 107 f.

Related to this particular liturgical meaning of time is also the wall-painting representation of Christ within the paten (Μελισμὸς) in the niche of the Sanctuary. In these representations Christ is not labeled ὁ τυθεὶς (the sacrificed one) but ὁ θυόμενος (the one being sacrificed),[21] that is, he who is continuously offered as sacrifice for us, precisely as it is accepted in worship again, wherein, according to the appropriate liturgical moment, μελίζεται καὶ διαμερίζεται ὁ ἀμνὸς τοῦ Θεοῦ ... (the lamb of God is cut into pieces and distributed . . . .). This example also indicates that Orthodox iconography not only places the divine events in the "continual present" and thus agrees even in this respect with worship, but also that this art, proven thus to be a purely liturgical art, directs the believer to the correct estimation of worship and to the interpretation of its content.

Thus, in conclusion, the removal in Orthodox worship of the limitations of the past, the present and the future and the regard of the divine events as ordered in eternity, which is lived in the present through them, is expressed in a characteristic manner through iconography, which again has raised the sacred persons and events to the continual present through the elements of its form.

---

[21] C. Kalokyris, *The Byzantine Wall-paintings of Crete,* 98, 126, also illus. LII, fig. 2, (θυόμενος in the Church of Kritsa).

CHAPTER FOUR

Main Directions and Presuppositions
for a Renaissance of Orthodox Iconography

1. *Western Models in Orthodox Art*

There are mainly three characteristic directions observed during our century in Orthodox painting, either presupposing or ignoring the essential character of Orthodox art and particularly its direct connection with worship—as developed in the previous chapters.

The first, chronologically older, direction (beginning already in the years of the Greek nation's domination by the Turks), is characterized by *the direct copy of Western models,* often with a simplification of them.[1] Icons of Christ and *especially of the Theotokos* were executed on the basis of these models (Raphael, Titian). There are fewer copies of scenes from the life of the Saviour among us. Primarily we have copies of the Annunciation (Botticelli, Raphael, Credi), of the Birth of Christ (Lippi, Ribera), of the Last Supper (Leonardo da Vinci, Tiepolo), of the prayer at Gethsemane (el Greco), of the icon "Behold the Man" (that is, mainly icons of the Νυμφίος, such as those of Cigoli, Golzius, and especially of Guido Reni), of the Crucifixion (as those of Donatello, el Greco, and others), of the deposition from the Cross (Raimondi, el Greco, Rembrandt), of the Resurrection (Fra Bartolommeo, Corn, Cort, and others), of the Supper at Emmaus (Rembrandt, Bellini), of the Ascension (as with the distorted and so often repeated copy of the Transfiguration of Raphael in the Vatican Museum),[2] etc.

2. *Supposed "Correction" of the Byzantine Models*

The second direction, dating from the 17th century and propagated mainly from the time of the independence of the Greek nation, is characterized by *the attempt to correct* the old Byzantine models on the basis of the methods of European art.[3] That

---

[1] See Prolegomena.

[2] See also p. 26. That is, Christ of the Transfiguration of Raphael is altered into a Ἀναλαμβανόμενον, (Ascension).

[3] It is the Scuola Bizantina Migliorata.

is, genuine Byzantine iconographic works were taken and altered *to be more natural* (natural mature beauty, anatomy, design, perspective, etc.) in order to satisfy contemporary aesthetic conceptions. Usually such "corrected" (!) works are large icons on the iconostasion of Christ and the Theotokos (Despotikai), the Platytera, the Pantocrator on the dome, the four Evangelists, and icons of the feast-day saints. But even in the Dodekaorton there are such "corrections." L. Thirsch, who did the wall-paintings in the Russian church of Athens; L. Seitz, who painted the icons on the iconostasion of the Metropolis Church of Athens; Thirsch's student S. Hatziyiannopoulos, who has worked in the churches of St. Irene and Hrysospiliotissa of Athens; and their senior K. Fanellis, who attempted decorations in the Metropolis Church of Athens, in St. Eleutherius (Little Metropolis), in the Romve church, and in others, are among us the most significant representatives of such a direction. Naturally, the importance of these churches, and the photographing and wide circulation of the designs of L. Thirsch, contributed greatly to the propagation of this style.

3. *Return to the Models of Orthodox Tradition.*
The Unity of Worship. The Oppositions.

But the two directions mentioned above indicate complete ignorance of the character and the essence of Orthodox iconography, and already during the last decades they have begun to be abandoned due to the wider flowering in Greece and in other foreign countries of Byzantine studies and, more specifically, of Byzantine art in general.[4] The study of this art is very lively today in the universities. The International Byzantinological Conferences continually verify its significance, and exhibit and promote its problems. Particular exhibitions of Byzantine and post-Byzantine icons initiate the public into its character. Research and the splendid publication of its monuments (as of the mosaics of Hagia Sophia in Constantinople, of the wall-paintings of the Pareklesion in the Church of St. Saviour in the Chora in the same city, of the wall-paintings of Castelseprio near Milan, etc. have attraced the admi-

---

[4] Regarding the movement in Greece see our study Νεώτεραι πρόοδοι τῆς Χριστιανικῆς καὶ Βυζαντινῆς Ἀρχαιολογίας (New Advances in Christian and Byzantine Archaeology) in Θεολογία, vol. 31, sec. I (Athens, 1960), 23-24.

ration of advanced theological and artistic circles throughout the world. And with us the Law "regarding Antiquities," which protects the Byzantine monuments, has given the right to the commission of Restorations of the Ministry of National Education[5] to protect, to clean, and to promote the Byzantine paintings of the country. Through the daily worthy results achieved in this service by the archaeologists commissioned to work in this connection and through the resulting publications,[6] the exceptional significance of this traditional art is manifested, while at the same time it is demonstrated that it constitutes the assured presupposition for the flourishing of a contemporary neo-Orthodox iconography.

A consequence of this whole current was the appearance of Orthodox iconographers, who understood the danger which this tradition itself was running (that is, through the abandonment and the distortion of a fundamental element of worship) and who turned with great zealousness to the Byzantine models. *This return to the source, to the venerable Orthodox Byzantine iconographic tradition* characterizes the third direction, and is true of our contemporary iconography. Today, panel icons and wall-paintings are done widely in Greece on the basis of genuine original models of Orthodox art. The names of notable iconographers are well-known: F. Kontoglou (plate 23), D. Pelekakis, Ag. Asteriades, S. Papanikolaou, S. Vasiliou, St. Kartakis (plates 25, 26, 27, 28, 29) and others. Even in Europe and America they have begun to paint iconographies of the Orthodox style. We note that recently (1959) students of F. Kontoglou were invited and went to Chevetogne, Belgium, where they painted the walls of the monastery church (and are already working on the crypt). In America they have started making Byzantine icons, mosaics, and wall-paintings, but the painters here are still lacking the theological presuppositions of Orthodox iconography. They simply copy works of other iconographers of

---

[5] Unfortunately, today (1965) the antiquities and the Byzantine monuments of Greece are no longer under the supervision of the Ministry of Education, but of another Ministry. Thus, the highest spiritual supervision of the State is no longer exercised upon them through competent authorities.

[6] Besides the independent studies see the Minutes of the Archaeological Society of Athens, and A. Orlandos, Τὸ Ἔργον τῆς ᾽Αρχαιολογικῆς ῾Εταιρίας, (passim), (The Work of the Archaeological Society).

Byzantine style. In the Balkan States, we mention the lively movement in Serbia regarding the Byzantine tradition. The Byzantine wall-paintings of this country are feverishly cleaned of oxidation and mouldiness, others with manifold damages are restored or, by removal from the walls, are taken to museums, while a multitude of studies and color editions of them are being published. In this country[7] there have also appeared studios whose works are inspired by the strict tradition of iconography.

What characterizes this third direction of contemporary iconography is the more or less strict adherence to the old models and to the often imitative repetition of these, resulting from a reaction against the two previous directions (pl. 24). The Orthodox believer who enjoys Orthodox art truly rejoices when he sees in the iconographic compositions appearing today in Orthodox churches, the effort being made to revive the Byzantine tradition of iconography. And he is inwardly satisfied as he verifies that one of the elements of worship—which was either deformed or driven out of the churches because of the vicissitudes after the Fall of Constantinople and replaced by another (element) foreign to Orthodoxy—is returning now to its rightful position. Thus, worship acquires a *unity of form* by the complete unity of its particular Byzantine (that is, Orthodox) elements. To the Byzantine formation of Orthodoxy's sacred texts (Liturgy, hymns, prayers), to the Byzantine performance of the Divine Liturgy and of the other liturgical rites, to the Byzantine magnificence of the external appearance of the celebrating clergy, to the architectural space of Byzantine tradition (the Byzantine church) in which the worship unfolds, and to the music, finally, to which the hymns are sung, there is added again in our days also Byzantine iconography. Certainly it is not necessary to say what significance there is in the removal of the disintegration of these essential elements of Orthodox worship and in their unity of form.

For this whole contemporary movement it is of no consequence that certain backward people, out of ignorance of the value of our iconography, still oppose it. Undoubtedly not out of an evil

---

[7] We have already said that the best of these are works of Greek iconographers (whose names are noted by Greek inscriptions), or of their pupils. See p. 64, note 81.

intention, these opponents of Byzantine painting,[8] who are often also under the influence of the naturalistic aesthetics of photographs,[9] only kindle by their whole attitude the zeal of those initiated and encourage them on to wider research and to the en-

---

[8] These people, even in their ignorance, become perhaps—in a particular sense—contemporary iconoclasts, not because they contend—anything but — in principle and intention any form of icons and, more generally, the ideas of icons (as the iconoclasts in the strict sense did of old), but because they oppose the icons of Byzantine style out of ignorance that these alone are, in the Orthodox sense, icons (rather *the icons*), that is, those to which the Orthodox Faith has been connected. For the sake of elucidation it is necessary to add the following also: The Orthodox *icon* is always understood as an anti-naturalistic presentation of the sacred persons, as we have seen; that is, as an attempt to render through art mainly the divine (for Christ) or the spiritual and deified (for the saints) character which appears in human form. Therefore, the Orthodox icon is concerned with the spiritual and not the individual character of the represented persons. And since the τιμὴ ἐπὶ τὸ πρωτότυπον διαβαίνει (honor passes through to the prototype) and not alone to the icon itself, according to the known formula of the seventh Ecumenical Council (this is actually a phrase of St. Basil the Great from his treatise on the Holy Spirit, Migne, *P.G.* 38, 149, incorporated in the doctrinal formula of the Seventh Ecumenical Council found in Mansi, *Sacrorum Conciliorum nova et amplissima Collectio*, XIII, 380), the believer must be assisted by the form of the icon to apprehend this prototype, that is, the sacredness of the represented person and to guide "through him the mind to the knowledge of God" (δι' αὐτοῦ ὁ νοῦς πρὸς τὴν θεογνωσίαν), (Synodicon of Orthodoxy, in *Triodeon*, ed. Apostolici Diaconia, 145). This is the δι' εἰκόνων τῆς ἀληθείας βεβαίωσις (verification of truth through the icons), included in the Synodicon (*Ibid.*, page 145). It is under this meaning that the Church saw the iconoclastic opposition to the icons in the eighth century, and it is with this same meaning that she restored them. The Church regarded such a work not as a merely typical thing (external, decorative), but as a question of the essence of Orthodoxy. That the Church connected the essence of Orthodoxy with this kind of icon is clearly seen from the fact that she regarded the victory of the icons as the *victory of Orthodoxy* and named the Sunday of "Orthodoxy" in commemoration.

[9] These people, influenced by the lithographic icons of the West (which, as we said, have not a dogmatico-liturgical character, but only a decorative one) understand the sacred icons in the same manner as the portraits and the photographic representations. But through such so-called icons of *naturalness*, it is not possible that οἱ θεώμενοι διανίστανται πρὸς τὴν τῶν πρωτοτύπων μνήμην τε καὶ ἐπιπόθησιν (the spectators depart toward the memory of and yearning for the prototypes) (Mansi, *op. cit.*, 380), because here certainly the point is "remembrance" of them as divine and not as worldly persons.

lightenment of their opponents. There are others, however, who openly recognize the value of this traditional art and who appreciate and enthusiastically salute this movement in the bosom of Orthodoxy. But these, again, are opposed to or at least are reserved in following the line of many iconographers, that is, from regarding the art of the past as an *already perfected* form, or in other words, as an unchangeable ideal of universal validity which can, through a mechanical repetition, be offered to move as of old the people of today. These reserved people serve, through their position, determined by superior motives, the known dialectical pattern of *thesis and antithesis,* from which the *synthesis* will indisputably come, that is, the newer artistic synthesis of form (for the point here concerns the form and not the content of iconography), which will renovate the old form without the change of its essence.

4. *The Evolutionary Element in the Tradition of Orthodox Iconography*

Actually we also believe that the enthusiasm of the artist-iconographers of this movement to promote the Byzantine iconography by copying or by slight modification of the old models does have the advantage of bringing the public closer to the spiritual nature of traditional iconography. At the same time, however, this enthusiasm overlooks a fundamental principle of art, which is precisely that art evolves continually and does not remain indifferent to its period. That is, it must become known—as we have written also at another time[10]—that Byzantine painting, as a true art, *always attempts* to express and never expresses *absolutely* its subjects. In such an effort precisely lies also its wealth; in the apparent weakness lies its power and great value. The attempt for expression presupposes a continual artistic drive to externalize and consequently a living organism unceasingly being so manifested and not relying upon past achievements. It is precisely this which deprives its works of staticism, which would otherwise result from any already completed artistic form. Hence the known periodical "renaissances" of Byzantine art (in the time of Justinian, the Macedonian emperors, the Comneni, the Palaeologi, the 16th century Cretan, and the current one in our days for its

---

[10] *The Birth of Christ in Byzantine Art,* 100, note 3.

theoretical study in Europe and America and for its practical exercise by painters) and its continual enrichment.[11]

The preferences of our iconographers in Greece who desire the revival of Byzantine iconography are turned partly to the art of the Palaeologi (with almost exclusive imitation of the so-called "Macedonian"[12] style, and rarely or none at all of the so-called "Cretan" style),[13] and partly to a combination of this art with that of the Macedonians and the Comneni—on the part of fewer artists —while more of them combine it with the art after the Fall of Constantinople (plates 30, 31, 32).

But these preferences (and certainly other related ones) of the contemporary iconographers—indicating their restlessness and equated to an expression through their art of the Byzantine tradition, whose vision lives in the depths of their hearts—are not enough for a real renaissance of iconography. We do not think that this renaissance can be achieved by the imitation of even the best Palaeologian or other works of Byzantine painting. Much more we believe that it is not a contribution to this renaissance to repeat in contemporary churches unyielding bodies, to paint anti-anatomical excesses and inaccurate designs (under the pretense especially of anti-realism), or forms intensely stylized, or faces and naked parts in the color of unmixed ochre (almost yellow!), etc. These constitute a misunderstanding of the meaning of Byzantine art as well as of art in general. It is one thing to interpret historically and to *justify* Byzantine art and another thing to repeat its self-same works without a change of substance toward the spirit of the people for whom they are destined. An art—

---

[11] Analogous is also the *attempt of expression* undertaken by Byzantine ecclesiastical poetry—as itself a true art—which confesses the unattainability, through its means, of the *absolute* praising of God. Cf. ῞Υμνους ὑφαίνειν συντόνως τεθιγμένους ἐργῶδες ἐστιν (It is very toilsome to weave hymns of perfection); likewise cf. the known: Ἀπορεῖ πᾶσα γλῶσσα εὐφημεῖν πρὸς ἀξίαν (Every tongue is at a loss to acclaim worthily), etc.

[12] Regarding this style see Millet, *Recherches sur l'iconographie*, 688-690; Dalton, *East Christian Art* (Oxford, 1925), 237 f.; Sotiriu, "Die byzantinische Malerei des XIV Jahrh. in Griechenland" in Ἑλληνικὰ (Athens, 1928), 95-113; Muratoff, *La peinture byzantine*, 149 f.; C. Kalokyris, *The Byzantine Wall-paintings of Crete*, 167; Xyngopoulos, *Catalogue*, 3 f.

[13] See in relation to this style my work, *The Byzantine Wall-paintings of Crete*, 167-177, where there is a related bibliography.

97

and especially an art in the service of the Church—must never ignore the whole spiritual climate of contemporary man, just as the leaders of the Church do not ignore this when, for example, they contemporize the sermon to the needs of the times. But even the history of our iconography teaches this. The form of the art of the catacombs was one; it was another under Justinian; another under the Macedonians; another under the Palaeologi; another in the post-Byzantine period,[14] as we have said above. That is to say, that while the art during all the periods remained *one* in essence and in spiritual content, its form was contemporized, its style underwent evolution, its representations were enriched[15]—precisely as it happens today with the sermon which remains in essence Christo- centric, even though it is enriched with new scientific and psychological facts which contemporize its form without ever changing its traditional ecclesiastical character.

The examples of two great painters of Orthodoxy are enough, we think, to convince us on the above issues, that is, the work of Michael Damascenos and Theophanes (the first constituting a milestone for the portable icons and the second for the wall-paintings).[16] Both of these men remained faithful to the spirit of Byzantine iconography (and particularly to the Palaeologan), even though both of them[17] received in their work elements of the Renaissance which, however, they subjected and entirely assimilated by their strong artistic personality. Both of them achieved, through the transubstantiation of their borrowed elements and of their unified feeling of form (which always remained Byzantine), absolute unity in their works, while at the same time they introduced a revitalized tradition familiar to the spirit of the times. The example of Damascenos and Theophanes was followed by other iconographers, with results of course related to the capabilities which each artist disposed for such a fertile union. Moreover, two centuries before Damascenos and Theophanes Manuel Panselenos rejuvenated the Orthodox iconography and

---

[14] For a related comparison see plates 1, 2, 5, 7, 10, 13, 15, 17, 20.

[15] That enrichment is meant which concerned elements not contradicting the dogma and the whole nature of iconography.

[16] C. Kalokyris, *The Byzantine Wall-paintings of Crete,* 176, 177.

[17] Damascenos also executed icons of an apparent Italianized style (probably in the period before his maturity), perhaps according to the desire of his employers.

became its great milestone, through the reception of realistic elements—in agreement with the whole spirit of the fourteenth century—which, however, he included in his work by a marvelous manner, assimilating and idealizing them without ever changing the austere character of Orthodox art.

5. A Fundamental Presupposition for the Real Renaissance of Iconography. The Dangers. The Leadership Role of the Church.

From what has been said above it is inferred that for an essential renaissance the first thing needed today is a concentrated study of the whole character of our iconography. Second, a research, characterized by much discretion and "fear of God," into those indisputably worthy and related elements from the contemporary artistic spirit can only bring a new breath of life to iconography — without the least change of its age-old character. We say that these newer elements are required only for this new breath in iconography because the renaissance will come from within, that is, *from the powers of this very same iconography,* which, however, will be strengthened, revived, and contemporized[18] by the inoculation of these artistically acknowledged and healthy orthodox elements. This is not an easy task, or a task of any one person, nor is it achieved from one day to the next. Much time will be required, of course, but first must come the knowledge of the essence of Byzantine iconography and the complete apprenticeship of the iconographers in the Byzantine original models—these inexhaustible springs for the great inspirations.

In a contrary situation, the systematic "selection" and repetition of the classical models of iconography will lead, through fruitless "eclecticism," to a *formalism,* which is so dangerous for the life of art. Formalism will present nothing else except dry copies, often transferred and placed in a space unsuited to the kind and the dimensions of the copies. Art is thus in danger of receiving the form of a mechanical and lifeless repetition of the same things, in precisely the same manner that works of great painters of the Renaissance are repeated by novice copyists in the museums

---

18 We think that the meaning of this term is here quite clear. It does not have a worldly meaning at all.

of Europe. This procedure, however, if it does not lead to an artistic decline, will perhaps cultivate the spirit *of growing old again* and not the spirit *of renaissance* in Orthodox art.

But here we must note something else. The current toward the traditional iconography which is increasing daily, the search for icons of Byzantine style started by many private persons and foreigners and especially tourists, has created among us a certain "fashion" for the Byzantine art. This "fashion," however, lowers Byzantine art from the high and purely artistic level, on which iconography is placed by the real artists, to the common vulgarity of the everyday market place. Painters of mediocre quality and, of course, of doubtful purposes hurry to satisfy the demands of this fad. These painters do not possess the special capability in Byzantine art and the necessary preparatory instruction, but for the sake of profit, they masquerade themselves and change *from worldly painters one day to Byzantine iconographers the next* (!). This is done under the danger of creating among us, little by little, a certain kind of the so-called *Madonneri*,[19] but of course of a lower quality than they were. These painters may be able to impress the crowds and, of course, the tourists with their well-made copies, but in reality they do damage, through their artless works of "industrialization," to the creations truly inspired by the tradition and to the essential cultivation of the people's understanding to apprehend the real quality of true Orthodox art. But it should be clear that there must be no confusion between this fad and the great movement of a truly exalted nature for Byzantine studies, nor between these artisans and the real iconographers,[20] whose works show indisputably the spiritual struggle of true artists and who are actually challenged by the sources of the sacred art of the Church. These artists of higher quality (as well as their pupils and other younger followers), regardless of their preferences for Byzantine art of the different periods from personal convictions and idiosyncrasies, are worthy of every honor.

---

[19] Not exactly as such. *Madonneri* were called those artisans of a usually mediocre quality in the 16th and 17th centuries in Italy and especially in Venice, who copied mainly Byzantine icons of the Theotokos (Madonna), which were much in demand and with which they made many profits. For Greek *Madonneri* see G. Gerola, *Monumenti Veneti nell' isola di Creta*, II, 312.

[20] Some of their names we mentioned above.

Through their return to the genuine Byzantine and post-Byzantine models, these artists have achieved the assured presupposition, which, little by little and with the help of the other elements mentioned, will lead to the new renaissance of Orthodox iconography.

In order to accelerate this very much desired renaissance and to guard it from possible false influences which slow it down, it is necessary that the Church receive again this art essentially under her leadership. Advanced Schools of Orthodox Iconography under the direction of the Church are necessary for today. Great artists like Damascenos, Theophanes, Tzanes, Skoufos, and a multitude of others did not come out of secular studies, but out of the bosom of the Church.[21] In these schools, parallel to the technique of iconography, its style, and its figures, there will also be the teaching of the history of Worship, Liturgies, and the fundamentals of Dogmatics and Christian Aesthetics (as e.g. the architectural space of the church in relationship to the iconographic patterns), and especially the relationship of all these to the iconography.

Since Orthodox iconography is indisputably and especially connected with the worship and the tradition of the Orthodox Church, it is up to the Church not only to enlighten her people about this relationship, but also to inform the Ecumenical Movement and to promote widely in it even this inheritance of hers which is of such a unique nature and significance.

---

[21] Michael Damascenos had his workshop most probably in the monastery of Vrontissi in Crete; Theophanes was a monk; Emmanuel Tzanes and Philotheos Skoufos were priests.

EPILEGOMENA

The examination of the form and the content of Orthodox iconography, undertaken in this study, defined its essence, which is constituted by the attempt to express the *holy*, which again is artistically served by the aesthetic category of the "sublime,"[1] arousing amazement and awe. Thus, it has become clear that Orthodox art is evaluated οὐκ ἀπὸ τῆς διαπλάσεως οὐδ' ἀπὸ τοῦ χρώματος, ἀλλ' ἀπὸ τῆς διακονίας (not from the form, nor from the color, but from the service it renders)[2] primarily to the sublime ideals of the Faith. To ignore this principle is a fundamental error in the study of this art.

It was noted in following that this "service" defines this art more particularly as an art of the *doctrine* and the *depth* of the sublime *Orthodox Theology,* and as a *liturgical art,* or, in one word, an art inseparably connected with Orthodox worship.[3]

---

[1] Christos Androutsos, Ψυχολογία (Athens, 1934), 306. The late author notes characteristically: Τὸ ὑψηλὸν εἶναι ἡ αἰσθητοποίησις τῆς ἰδέας τοῦ ἀπείρου, ὡς τοιοῦτον δὲ ἐκπλήσσει μᾶλλον καὶ ἐμποιεῖ θαυμασμὸν ἢ ἀρέσκει... (the sublime is making perceivable the idea of the infinite and, as such, amazes and creates admiration rather than satisfaction . . .). Cf. more generally F. Unbuch, *Der Begriff des Erhaben,* 1898. Th. Lipps, *Ästhetik,* 2, ed. 2a, 1921, 76. P. A. Michelis, Αἰσθητικὴ θεώρηση τῆς Βυζαντινῆς Τέχνης (Aesthetic Survey of Byzantine Art), (Athens, 1946).

[2] St. John Chrysostom; see chapter one of this study, p. 13 f.

[3] Thus, our study constitutes an archaeological, aesthetic, and dogmatic interpretation of our painting, and, through such research, a contribution to Orthodox worship.

The given *archaeological* facts determined for us the historical evolution of iconography in the beginning as symbolic, after that as historical, as dogmatic, and later as narrative art. The given facts of the catacombs (fish, lamb, good shepherd, etc.), of the erection of the churches following the triumph of Christianity, particularly of the formation of iconographic cycles after the iconoclastic controversy, and of the dogmatic exaltation of the iconography became presuppositions for the interpretation of this sacred art. The archaeological interpretation, moreover, was determined by the knowledge, through archaeology, of the monuments of painting of the Christian world (Orthodox and non-Orthodox), the comparisons made between them, and the verification of the periods of painting and of the forms of iconography.

The *aesthetic* interpretation of our iconography was composed, from

Following, it was said that in order to respond to these purposes, defining its content, our iconography adopted an analogous form, that is, it created works of a particular morphological conception, removing the believer from the natural reality and leading him into the regenerated world of Divine Grace. This idea is expressed by the reconciled representation of the space and by the whole anti-realistic style applied to the faces and the objects of iconography.

It was later affirmed that even though our iconography is an art purely idealistic, it does not, however, ignore even the realistic element which especially became its declarative characteristic during the period of the Palaeologi. But this realism then and

---

the viewpoint of the content of art, not only by the certification of the category of holiness as one of its ideals (in contrast to the beauty of the ancients), but also, from the morphological viewpoint, by the thorough examination of its attempt to render through it the sublime spiritual atmosphere of the "regenerated" world of Divine Grace. This expression of form was defined both by the reasonable use of colors in painting the sacred figures, enclosed within characteristic contours, and by the rendition of their mass and their details through the richer colors and chiaroscuro. Similarly, through the aesthetic interpretation, we examined the idealistic stylization (of ears, nose, eyes, etc.) and the purposeful avoidance of the anatomical truth (bodies, fingers, etc.), by which the "divine change," that is, the spiritualization of the sensory organs is achieved. It was also verified that the spirituality of iconography is expressed also by the aesthetics of the foldings of the garments, which is manifest in geometrical rhythmic stylization, by the ὑπέρθεσις (superposition) of the figures, the ἀνεστραμμένη προοπτικὴ (inverted perspective), and finally by the realism which, however, possesses a ὑπερ-προσωπικὸν (supra-personal) character. These ἀντίθετα (opposites, contrasts) to the natural facts and perhaps entirely παράδοξα (paradoxical) (or even apparently illogical things) of the aesthetics of Orthodox painting should not in the least surprise anyone when the idea which they express has been made known. They are, undoubtedly, in agreement with the spiritual ideals of the Church, and they remind us of the related declaration of St. Paul that ὁ Θεὸς εὐδόκησε διὰ τῆς μωρίας τοῦ κηρύγματος (it pleased God by the foolishness of preaching) to accomplish His work of saving the world (I Cor. 1:21). Of course, this means what *seems* like foolishness to the "wisdom" of men.

The *dogmatic* interpretation of Orthodox iconography, generally speaking, was founded on the relation of its works to the whole of Orthodox theology, the Orthodox doctrine, and the related opinions of the Fathers of the Church. This interpretation was dictated by the meaning which is held by Christ in the dome (Pantocrator, Father and Son together—"consubstantial," Creator, Saviour, Judge), by the Platytera Theotokos in the

in every period of Byzantine art did not constitute a slavish imitation of living models, as happened in the religious art of the West, which received natural persons as models for the representation of its saints. In our iconography this realism is included in its whole transcendent climate; it is idealized, ennobled, and transformed into an element of sublime expression.

Even though this entire study affirmed the relation of iconography to worship, a special chapter underlined also this bond and developed more particularly the fact that iconography makes perceivable and is a commentary to whatever is "mystically" enacted in worship. Thus, Orthodox iconography was presented as an inseparable element of Orthodox worship. But the relation of iconography to worship was shown also by our indication of that common acceptance of the concept of time, according to which, "liturgically," the limits of the past, the present, and the future are lifted so as to regard the past and the future as a direct present. In this continual present and through the elements of its form, our iconography depicted the sacred persons and events. Thus, it becomes understandable why the historical achievements

---

quarter-sphere of the niche in the Sanctuary (an expression of the Incarnation of God the Logos), and by the Saints in the remaining space of the church (citizens of Heaven, "clothed in glory not of earthly things but of the Heavenly things"). But particular dogmatic interpretation is found in the representation of the Saviour. That is to say, the Orthodox art does not represent Him as only a beautiful man according to nature (as Western art does), for this would be a Nestorian heresy, since by the over-emphasis of the natural element the idea of the one nature (the human) only would be projected of the "dual-natured" God-Man. But the Saviour's icon represents, in a dogmatic sense, the *Prosopon* of God the Logos (in whom the hypostatic union of the two natures took place), that is to say, that ideal form in which His Divinity and His ὁμόθεος (co-divine) and ὁμότιμος (co-honorable) holy Body is exalted. The dogmatic significance of iconography is seen also in the representation of two fundamental sacred scenes, that is, the Crucifixion and the Resurrection. The first does not insist on representing a tragic human drama (as it happens in Western art), but is raised to the expression of the τετελεσμένης (completed) sacrifice upon the Cross («τετέλεσται»), of the mystery of the κενώσεως τοῦ ἀκενώτου (emptiness of the inexhaustible) Logos. The second, through the type of the Descent into Hades, expresses a whole dogmatic theology about the achieved work of Christ through the Resurrection (catholic, universal redemption), which is not in the least bit rendered by the icon showing the Lord rising from a sarcophagus tomb—an icon of Italian inspiration and unsuited to the Orthodox tradition.

of this sacred art speak in the same manner to the hearts of the believers of today and of tomorrow just as they spoke also to the believers of the past. In this way we understand also why these *supra-temporal* classical works of Byzantine art are not repeatable, precisely as the Parthenon and the Hagia Sophia are not.

Moreover, the main directions of iconography were presented, and especially the direction during our days, which is characterized by the return to the Orthodox painting tradition, that is, to the models of Byzantine and post-Byzantine iconography. Besides the danger of formalism, on the one hand (to which the emerging tendency of true artists to imitate and repeat classical models of Byzantine art may lead) and the "Byzantine fashion," on the other hand, which attracts mainly mediocre artisans (and distorts the artistic sense of many people through the lifeless and usually "ill-treated" copies), it was also sufficiently emphasized that artists and iconographers of superior motives have found, through the concentrated study of the sources, the way for the renaissance of our art. Similarly, it was pointed out that for this renaissance it is necessary to take into account also the whole spiritual climate of our period as well as the possible related elements of the contemporary artistic world—in accordance with the example of the great iconographers of Orthodoxy, such as Panselenos, Damascenos, and Theophanes. These elements, with their new breath of life, will revitalize the body of iconography, whose revival, however, will be attributed always to its inherent liveliness and spiritual power.

Finally, it was noted that the success of the whole contemporary movement can be guaranteed by the responsible Orthodox Church, by placing this art once again under her guardianship, by establishing "Advanced Schools of Orthodox Iconography," and by enlightening the people, through competent Byzantinologists, about its essentially doctrinal content, its spiritual form, and its particular contribution to worship in general.

LIST OF PLATES

21 *St. John the Forerunner.* Icon from the Monastery of Gonia, Crete.

22 *Christ Pantocrator.* Portable icon from the Monastery of Gonia, Crete.

23 Section of a recently executed wall-painting of *The Ascension,* in the Church of St. Nicholas at Kato Patesia, Athens. By the icon painter Fotis Kontoglou.

24 *The Reclining Christ-child, ("Anapeson").* Copy by the monk Theophilos of a work of Panselenos at the Church of the Protaton, Mount Athos.

25 *Christ Pantocrator.* A recent wall-painting on the cupola of the Church of St. Menas in Heracleion, Crete, by Stylianos Kartakes.

26 *The Prophet Jeremiah.* Contemporary wall-painting in the Church of St. Menas, Heracleion, Crete, by Stylianos Kartakes.

27 *Interior of a contemporary Orthodox Church* painted in the Byzantine tradition. (Kartakes).

28 *Interior of St. Menas,* in Crete. Work of Kartakes.

29 *The Sanctuary and the Eastern Arch* of the church in the preceding plate.

30 *St. John the Forerunner.* Contemporary portable icon, by a painter from Mount Athos.

31 *The Three Children in the Furnace.* Copy of the painting at Protaton, Mount Athos, by the monk Father Seraphim.

32 *Angel.* Detail of the preceding plate.

33 *The Ascension of Christ.* Mosaic from the cupola of St. Sophia of Salonica. Ninth century.

34 *The Archangel Michael.* Icon from the monastery of Chilandari, Mount Athos. Fourteenth century.

35 *Angels.* Wall-painting from Perivleptos of Mistra. Fourteenth century.

36 *Theotokos the Infant-carrier, and St. Nicholas.* Wall-painting from the Monastery of Docheiariou, Mount Athos. Sixteenth century.

37 *Saints, (monks).* Wall-painting from the Monastery of Docheiariou, Mount Athos. Sixteenth century.

38 *The Resurrection of Christ, ("Touch me not!").* Icon by Michael Damaskenos. Sixteenth century.

PLATE 1

PLATE 2

PLATE 3

PLATE 4

PLATE 5

PLATE 6

PLATE 7

PLATE 8

PLATE 9

PLATE 10

PLATE 11

PLATE 12

PLATE 13

PLATE 14

PLATE 15

PLATE 16

PLATE 17

PLATE 18

PLATE 19

PLATE 20

PLATE 21

PLATE 22

PLATE 23

PLATE 24

PLATE 25

PLATE 26

PLATE 27

PLATE 28

PLATE 29

PLATE 30

PLATE 31

PLATE 32

PLATE 33

PLATE 34

PLATE 35

PLATE 36

PLATE 37

PLATE 38